The Uncommon Journey of a Common Man

by
Gary Owens

Copyright © 2008 by Gary Owens

ISBN 0-7414-5089-5

Published by:

PUBLISHING.COM

1094 New DeHaven Street, Suite 100
West Conshohocken, PA 19428-2713
Info@buybooksontheweb.com
www.buybooksontheweb.com
Toll-free (877) BUY BOOK
Local Phone (610) 941-9999
Fax (610) 941-9959

Printed in the United States of America

Printed on Recycled Paper

Published November 2008

Table of Contents

I

Foreword

You are fortunate!! Whether you have purchased this book or received it as a gift, you are about to embark on an adventure into the life and times of Gary Owens, a most unique person. Gary shares his personal encounters with some of the most famous and notorious figures of the 20th century and in such detail that the book is almost impossible to put down until the last page. Exciting, funny and sometimes tragic are the pages. It is like sitting with him and listening to someone "unfold in thought and paint his life."

An exceptional songwriter, guitarist, stained glass artist, singer and classic film critic and creative film producer are just some of the talents he possesses. He is so knowledgeable on so many subjects ~ thinking selfishly now ~ it seems unfair.

There are "fair weather friends" who are available at "their" convenience when you call and then there are "Friends" who are, at any moment, day or night, rain or shine, there for you when you need a friend the most. Gary Owens is that kind of friend and he makes me Blessed!!

Buzz Arledge
A Friend

Introduction

Ernest Hemingway was once asked, "How does one become a writer?" His reply was as curt as it was honest. "Hell, it's easy," he said, "you just attach the seat of your pants to the seat of your chair and write!" With those time tested words, I suppose anyone setting out to write a book must follow Hemingway's instructions to the letter. However, at some point the heart, mind, and soul must come into play, providing direction, depth, and purpose. It helps to have lived a little and traveled off the well beaten paths.

      The idea to write a book did not fall on me suddenly, like a ton of bricks but rather settled upon me ever so gently over a long period of time. Urged on by friends to write down some of my life experiences: one day I did! A few days later I added some more details. Soon I was compelled to write a little each day. *This* book is the result.

At first glance, you might think this book is primarily about me. It is not. I'm just one of the many characters: an observer and narrator, if you will. Without all the many *others*, I might as well have written a book about a man standing out in a field, with his hands in his pockets.

Others are the subjects of this writing. The people, their places, their times, and the events. Some happy. Many tragic. My association with them all can perhaps be credited to a fair amount of serendipity.*

As a young boy, I was always eager to seek out the colorful characters ~ the ones who make this world a more interesting place. I've continued with this approach throughout my life. And those colorful characters I mentioned, are everywhere to be found. Now and again, if you'll just stand still ~ they'll find you.

Gary Owens

*Horace Walpole coined the word serendipity in 1754. He formed the word on an old name for Sri Lanka: Serendip. The word was part of the title of a fairy tale, called **The Three Princes of Serendip**: "*as their highnesses traveled, they were always making discoveries, by accident, of things which they were not in quest of....*"

Chapter 1

Roots & Ties

The Illinois Territory was granted statehood in the year 1818. A few short years later my Great-Great-Great Grandfather, Joseph Owens, arrived in southern Illinois from Lynchburg, Tennessee. He settled in the town of Benton. Joseph had several children one of whom was a son named Logan, born in 1833. When the Civil War broke out in 1861, southern sympathy drove 28 year old Logan Owens, like many others, to head south and sign up with the Confederate Army. Pvt. Logan Owens was assigned to Company K, 17th Tennessee Infantry.

On December 31, 1862 he was wounded in the Battle of Stones River in Murfreesboro, Tennessee. The battle resulted in nearly 16,000 deaths, with several thousand more being wounded. On September 18, 1863 he again fought. This time in the battle of Chickamauga.

After his discharge from the service, Logan returned to Benton and married a young lady named Sarah Whaley. The union produced several children, one of whom was a son named Phelix, who had several sons, one named Edward. Edward had several children including a son named Frank. Frank is my father. At this writing he is 84 years old.

Figure 1: Here I'm holding my two year old son, Justin Logan Owens ~ Namesake and Great-Great-Great Grandson of Private Logan Owens.

Logan Owens died in 1908 at the age of 75. His obituary stated he was "a quiet and peaceable man." He is buried in the Masonic and Oddfellows Cemetery in Benton, Illinois.

In the summer of 2000, the Sons of the Confederacy awarded a Bronze Star to Logan Owens: *(Figure 1)*. My father's brother, my Uncle Felix, accepted the award on behalf of the entire family.

Valier Patch

I was born in 1949 in southern Illinois and grew up in a small coal mining settlement known as Valier Patch: population 50. This was the land of the infamous labor wars of the 1920s, between union coal miners and the scab strikebreakers. Both had left a lot of blood on the ground ~ along with the gangsters of Franklin and Williamson counties. One can only imagine a time when thousands of hooded Ku Klux Klan members clashed with bootleggers, while armed National Guardsmen patrolled the streets of many small towns, for the protection of the citizenry. Often the Protestant was pitted against the Catholic; the natural born against the foreign born.

"The Patch," as people call it, is about a quarter of a mile north of the village of Valier: population 662. There was always a broad line drawn between the two places. A lot of the Valier residents looked down their noses at folks from "The Patch."

Our home in Valier Patch sat within a thousand feet of the Valier Coal Mine. Each morning I awoke to the sound of the mine whistle blasting away. The mine whistle was prone to blow at any time, day or night. On those occasions people knew something was amiss at the mine. Families of the miners, along with the curious, would gather at the mine gate and wait for word from mine officials as to what was going on. All knew it was a disaster of some kind, some worse than others, often resulting in the death of one or more men. The waiting was a time of anguish.

When coal miners go to work, they ride a huge cage elevator about 700 feet straight down. They then hop on a small shuttle train and travel as much as ten miles in either direction. Anything can happen. The job is full of hazards, perhaps less today than years ago, but dangers still exist. The miners and their families have come to accept this.

Most of the folks in Valier Patch were retired coal miners of European origin: Italian, Polish, and Hungarian. Their lawns were manicured, and they had immaculate gardens wherein they grew their own vegetables. Most backyards had fruit cellars, which doubled as storm cellars. Many had small grape vineyards. They made and bottled their own wine. In the 1950s, there still existed a lot of customs and traditions brought over from the old country.

One neighbor, Eli Kosonavich, with his wife Louise, ran a small neighborhood grocery in Valier Patch. Eli made blood pudding from the blood of goats he butchered for meat. He would cut their throats and catch the blood in a large pot. This was placed over a smoldering fire. He would stir this, adding various condiments and spices until it began to coagulate. It was quite delicious in spite of its origin.

4

Another neighbor named Leonard Pinazzi was a film buff. He had built a large movie screen in his yard and a small building from where he would project movies. Another outbuilding was full of vintage 35mm films he had collected throughout the years: both silents and talkies. Each summer of my childhood, Leonard would on Friday nights, show several cartoons and a couple movies. All the kids in Valier Patch would gather there with drinks and grocery bags full of popcorn .

There was a junk dealer in Valier Patch who was years ahead of his time. In his shop you could find anything your heart desired. The place was owned and operated by a fellow named Emil Philipak. He was a little man, always chomping away on a cigar, and he had a voice which sounded a lot like someone picking up a badger with a pair of pliers. Pete's Tavern was where the old men gathered outside to drank beer and play boccie ball.

My family put out a large garden each spring, like all families did, and come harvest time we would do our canning. Green beans, tomatoes, and sauerkraut were canned. We'd freeze corn on the cob along with a head of beef my dad butchered each year.

We would wring chicken's necks by the dozens and dress them. A common sight people won't see today, are a half dozen headless chickens running around haphazardly in the backyard. Those would go into the old deep freeze as well.

Free Coal

During the winter months, my father, along with my brother Deon and I, would go to the coal yard with shovels and several empty bushel baskets. We would shovel up the coal which had fallen from the boxcars onto the tracks. A family friend worked for the mines at the time. After a boxcar was filled with coal, it was his job to ride it down the track, tightening the hand break along the way. He would then hop off and let the car collide into the collection of coal cars until a train had been made up. An engine would then come along and haul the 50 or so cars away. Often times, when he would see us down there with our shovels and baskets, he would just barely tighten the hand brake, so when the coal car hit it would send a lot more coal onto the ground. It meant more for us. We seldom ever paid for coal.

The Old Sesser Trail

Once a month, a covered wagon pulled by two horses would mosey past our house. An elderly brother and sister, who lived nearby, would be making the seven mile journey north, to the town of Sesser, to pick up provisions like flour and sugar. They lived in a house with no electricity, and like a lot of country folks in the 1950s, they still drew their water from a well. When I'd see them coming, I would run out and hop up on the back of their wagon and ride for a while. They didn't mind. I would usually hop off after a mile or so, but one day I stayed on and made the trip along the back roads, all the way to Sesser.

It was a real adventure for a kid, especially when traveling the three miles or so of dirt road. With not a single house in sight and no signs of civilization, it really felt like I was living back in the olden days when horse and wagon were the standard mode of travel. As we entered the town of Sesser, children ran behind the wagon waving and laughing. I supposed they were wishing they could ride up there with me. But this was my hour in the sun. I laughed and waved back at them.

When I returned home my mother hadn't a clue as to where I had been. Today if a child isn't heard from every 20 minutes or so the parents have a panic attack. 1959 wasn't just another time: it was another world.

Sometimes, during the summer months, my brother Deon and I would load up our army surplus backpacks and fill our canteens. We would then hike the 12 plus miles to our Grandparent's farm located in an area called "The Diggins." It consisted of a few small farms, a church, and an old one room schoolhouse. We'd stop off at houses along the way to refill our canteens. A large portion of the trip would be through an area known as the Big

Muddy Bottoms. It was made up of several hundred wooded acres, with the Big Muddy River cutting through it. I recall tagging along there, once or twice, with my Grandfather on coon hunts. An old logging road full of ruts and mud holes traversed "the bottoms," dotted with several small bridges consisting of nothing more than rough cut lumber placed across makeshift pillars. As of 1970, the Big Muddy Bottoms is at the bottom of Rend Lake. The Rend Lake Conservancy came in and ran my mother's people off in all directions. There was always talk of the great prosperity the lake would bring to the area. However, forty plus years hasn't presented much proof of it. After all was said and done, the farms of my kinfolk and all the others were not even earmarked for lake property. The government leases the land to corporate farming interests for crops.

A Noble Man

A man named Noble Montgomery: *(Figure 2)* lived near us. Noble was missing both arms, well above the elbows, one leg, and he was blind in one eye: all the result of a mining accident. The average person would have felt pretty handicapped but not Noble Montgomery. Noble had a reputation as a hard working, honest, and decent man. He raised three sons, Charlie, Wayne, and Jerry.

Figure 2: Noble Montgomery with his John: one of Grandchildren.

They grew up to have the same work ethic and good character as their father. At a distance, Noble was an inspiration to me. I was just a kid, but even then my young mind was conscious of these facts: life deals different hands to people, and people handle it all in different ways.

Knowing of Noble Montgomery made me think twice before whining about not being allowed to go or do or get. My father was a hard worker but then he had two good arms and two good legs, as did most other men. Noble Montgomery's ability to function beyond his physical limitations put a whole new spin on the words *can-do*. Noble moved through life with this mindset: not only was he **NOT** disabled but he was *able* to do anything. Noble Montgomery passed away in 1980.

9

Still, to this day, people speak respectfully of him. Noble's attitude of "wipe away the blood and sweat and keep moving," was passed down to his sons as well.

Jerry Montgomery, Noble's youngest, had contracted polio as a baby. Polio! A word kids today don't even know, but back in the fifties we small children were lined up and inoculated against the dreaded *polio*. Jerry walked with crutches, but like his father and brothers, he could do anything, including riding a beautiful Cushman Motor Scooter: *(Figure 3)*. I wanted that scooter from the first time I saw Jerry riding it; a few short years later, Noble held an auction on his farm. My father went, taking along my brother Deon and me. There was that scooter.

Figure 3:

A 1947 Cushman Motor Scooter. Model 62.

We begged dad to get it. He finally gave in, and we didn't even have to bid on it. Dad asked Noble how much he thought it might bring. Noble eyeballed my brother and me, standing there all anxious and said, "I'll take ten dollars for it."

10

Deon and I were the happiest kids in the world. We had not gotten some common ordinary run of the mill motor scooter, some little Vespa sounding like a bumble bee farting in a tin can, but rather a 1947 Model 62 Cushman Motor Scooter with a centrifugal clutch. It was blue and white. Back in those days, Cushman was the Harley Davidson of motor scooters and, it was all ours! It took a little work to get it running again but in no time, we were riding it around Valier Patch. A few times we rode it through the Big Muddy Bottoms, to our cousin's farm. They'd ride the scooter while we rode their horse.

One day I was riding the scooter with my brother on the back, when the throttle got stuck. We were traveling along at top speed, 45mph, and while attempting to stop by stomping at the brake pedal, the brakes went out. We were fast approaching the point where the road came to a T intersection at the blacktop. I was at the helm, so to speak, so I yelled back to Deon how I was going to stand up, and he was to pull the seat off and disconnect the spark plug wire, killing the engine. It was a great plan, considering the tension of the moment. When I stood up, Deon grabbed the seat and tossed it away. He reached in and pulled the spark plug wire, which then fell against his arm, sending an electric shock through him. His violent reaction to the electric shock caused the motor scooter to begin fishtailing in the loose gravel.

Of course, I was still standing and couldn't sit down because the seat was now gone. Deon had slid off the back end and was holding on for dear life, with his feet dragging in the gravel. Still moving at a good clip, the scooter swerved into a ditch. Then we hit a rock. It wasn't a large rock. Just big enough to finalize the ongoing catastrophe. The scooter went one way while Deon and I went the other. At first we didn't know who or what was hurt the most. The scooter wasn't complaining. It just lay there. We had no broken bones but several abrasions. We got the scooter out of the ditch and pushed it home. With a few adjustments here and there and a little WD40, we were soon back on the road again. A few years later we loaded the scooter onto our truck and hauled it to an auction barn. It brought just what we had paid for it: ten dollars.

The Great Owensini

I was ten years old when I sent off for a catalog of magic tricks: *"Vic Lawston's House of a Thousand Mysteries."* I would sit for hours looking through the catalog, daydreaming of someday becoming a great magician like Harry Houdini.

I scraped together fifty cents and placed an order. At last, the day came when the postman placed a small package in the mailbox, and my heart pounded. I ran to my room with the package and opened it. Here was what I had waited for. The mysteries of a thousand pyramids were revealed to me. Now with the flick of my fingers, I could pluck from the air: a rose! Then another and another and on and on: as many roses as I desired. I stood before a mirror practicing until I had it down perfect.

I took my new trick to school and astounded my friends with my talent. They begged me to show them how it was done, but I was true to the magician's code to never reveal a trick. I had to admit, I enjoyed the power I held over them. I created an act and would perform it in my bedroom night after night. I did card tricks and coin tricks and, of course, the rose trick. I had a cape, a wand, and a real silk top hat someone had given me. I found an old suitcase and created a logo on it's side with a fan of playing cards and the words: "The Great Owensini." Harry Houdini, the escape artist, was a hero of mine. I had worked a couple escape stunts into the act as well.

One day, Mr. Patchett, our home room teacher, asked if I'd put on a magic show for the class. I jumped at the chance. The next day I went to school carrying my little suitcase, and all the kids were anxious to see the big magic show. I began with a few simple sleight of hand tricks. They were impressed. After a couple card tricks and of course, the famous "rose from thin air" trick, I had them hooked. Then it came time to amaze my audience with my great escape from a rope and chain.

George Bradley and Tommy Griffin, two strapping big classmates, volunteered to tie me up, and they did a superb job. I hobbled out into the hallway, and in the privacy of the great hall I broke free of my bonds, and a short half minute later stepped back into the classroom to the applause and cheers of my adoring fans, which I now had in the palm of my hand.

Mr. Patchett then broadsided me with a suggestion: "Why not let a couple of the girls tie you up?" The boys chuckled at the mere silliness and futility of the idea, but I boldly accepted the challenge.

Judy Vercellino and Jo Dawn Smith stepped up to volunteer. They began to tie the rope and chain around and around. I knew I was in trouble the second the chain began to cut off the circulation to my hands. A great magician needs his hands you know. Judy and Jo Dawn must have put their hearts and souls into tying me up, as they did so much more aggressively than did George and Tommy. Again, I made my way into the hallway.

I was midway into a panic attack by the time Mr. Patchett closed the classroom door, leaving me out there in the hallway, with me knowing there wasn't a chance of freeing myself. I had wanted to turn to him at the last minute and tell him I didn't think I could get out of this mess of chain and rope. Still, I struggled. Soon I was running out of steam, but I was determined to not give up.

After what seemed like a big chunk of eternity, as my wrists were being rubbed raw, Mr. Patchett stuck his head out from the classroom and quietly asked, "Do you need some help?" I sheepishly responded with a humble, "Yes." He came out and tried to get me free but to no avail.

He then went to the furnace room and borrowed a pair of wire cutters from Coonie Patton, the school janitor. With Coonie and a couple others looking on, he performed the operation with the skill of a surgeon. The Great Owensini survived that day, and it was just a matter of time before I left magic far behind ~ to write poetry and songs.

Professor Grace Seiler

At about age nine, I asked my dad to build for me: a shoeshine box. I charged ten cents for a shoe shine. Once a week I would make the rounds in the neighborhood shining the shoes of the old gentlemen in Valier Patch. I'd go down to Pete's Tavern and watch the old men play boccie ball out back. I'd shine their shoes for a dime and fetch their beers for them. I got a nickel a trip.

I mowed the yards of the old folks in Valier Patch. I charged a dollar per lawn, no matter how big. When I wasn't performing chores for them, I would sit with them beneath their shade trees, listening to the stories of their lives, of their

15

hometowns back in the old country. They had   all come to America via Ellis Island. Many had met their spouses on the boat ride over. Once they had been processed into *America The Beautiful,* they made their way to the southern Illinois coalfields, which promised a life of gainful employment.

Life wasn't easy for these immigrants. The prejudices which existed among the natural born were great. The natural born being the ones whose ancestors, like mine, had traveled up from Tennessee and Kentucky in the early 1800s to settle the southern region of Illinois. With them came their moonshine stills and their many backward ways.

Many also brought their fears and suspicions of anyone who wasn't just like them, as well as the southern bible belt mentality of raising hell on Saturday night and singing in the pews on Sunday morning. The immigrants were all Catholic, though many were lapsed, while the natural born were protestant, mostly Baptist or Church of Christ. I grew up with such a glaring   difference: always a bone of contention.

There was one neighbor who stood out from all the others ~ Miss Grace Seiler: *(Figure 4)*. Miss Seiler was a Professor of English at East Carolina College in Greenville, North Carolina. Today it is called East Carolina University. She began her teaching career in economics at the Valier High School, and after a short time moved on to the College level. She retired from teaching in 1965.

Figure 4: Professor Grace Seiler in 1953 when she taught at Valier High School. She went on to greater things.

She taught nine months of the year and returned to Valier Patch each summer for a three month stay. The only time a taxicab ever came to Valier Patch was when Miss Seiler came home for the summer. She would hold up in her house with a couple five gallon bottles of fresh water and bags of fruit.

Her house: *(Figure 5)* sat in a grove of trees across the road from us. It was a two story farm house ~ white with green wooden shutters. Not those faux shutters like houses have today but real working shutters. The yard was grown over in weeds, and saplings grew everywhere.

There was a large red barn in the back. It had not been used in decades. Her father had built the house and barn with the timber from his own land.

Figure 5: The former home of Professor Grace Seiler. Valier Patch, Illinois.

My first recollection of Miss Seiler was when I was maybe 5 or 6 years old. A long black hearse was backed up to the front door of her home. Two men were removing a dead body from the house. The body was shrouded, on a gurney. A woman was hysterical; pining away at the top of her lungs. She attempted to throw herself upon the gurney, but others there prevented her from doing so. The hysterical woman was Miss Seiler. It was the day her "Papa" died.

Miss Seiler had always been a mystery to us, until one day she showed up on our doorstep in distress. It seemed a snake was climbing the trees in her yard, terrorizing and devouring all the baby birds. My father, with his .22 rifle; me and Deon in tow, followed her back home. Dad had only one bullet, and with a single shot he killed a large black snake as it crawled across the highest limb of a mighty oak. From that day on, the entire Owens family was welcomed into the secret world of Miss Grace Seiler. I would go visit her, and she would talk on subjects far over my young head, literature mostly, and I enjoyed the experience. She had books stacked throughout the house, and although the place smelled of mildew and mothballs, I visited frequently.

Years later, when I read Charles Dicken's "Great Expectations" and the various works of Edgar Allen Poe, I was reminded of Miss Seiler. Those writings held a special meaning for me, as I knew first hand, there really were people who lived among dust and decay ~ self exiled from the present to live in the past. It didn't matter whether the memories were bad or good ~ when it was all they had.

One day in 1966, I went to see Miss Seiler to ask if there were some tasks I might perform to earn some money. A couple friends, Brad White and David Hope and myself, were going to Huff's Recording Studio in nearby Christopher to make a record. Miss Seiler told me I could cut all the saplings in the front yard, which were quite sizable, and plentiful. Then I could mow the yard. I went to work and stayed at it all day. I cut, dragged, and stacked saplings and mowed her rock and root infested yard. At the end of the day Miss Seiler handed me a folded check. I thanked her and placed it in my shirt pocket. When I got home I discovered she had paid me the grand sum of $3.57. I wasn't upset. I knew she was a sweet old lady; a little eccentric. Considering my portion of the recording was going to be $2.50, I figured I had accomplished what I'd set out to do.

A couple years later, after I had moved away, I came home for a visit. My father asked me to help him do a favor for Miss Seiler. She was sick and had been staying in an upstairs bedroom of her home. There was a bedroom downstairs, with the bed on which her "Papa" had died many years prior. The bed had remained as it was from the day he died, unmade, with the impression of his head left upon the pillow. She wanted us to move an old refrigerator up those narrow steep stairs to her room. We complied with her wish.

It was a real chore getting the heavy bulky object up the stairs but we managed. The moment we set the fridge down in her room she said, "Oh no, take it back downstairs, it's too heavy for the floor." My father let her know in no uncertain terms, the fridge was staying right where it was.

Over the days, Miss Seiler's condition worsened. She developed a fever and became delirious. She refused to see a doctor. Then at the insistence of her brother, with whom she didn't get along with well, she went to the hospital. She was, to the amazement of my parents, declared *insane*! She was committed to the Anna Hospital for the Insane, in Anna, Illinois. Not for a moment did my parents believe her to be insane. I recall them raising the issue with the hospital's doctors. At the insistence of my parents, further investigation and tests revealed Miss Seiler was suffering with Rocky Mountain Spotted Fever, the result of a tick bite. She was treated and soon released.

I don't think she had much to do with her brother again, until the early 1980s, when she began to grow senile. At some point, the brother took over all of her personal and financial business.

Professor Grace Seiler spent her remaining days at a nursing home in nearby Sesser, where in 1988 she finally went to be with "Papa."

Over the years, the former home of Miss Grace Seiler has gone by the way of all neglected structures. We see them from time to time ~ ghosts from the past, sitting off the highways in the middle of bean fields. Without proper attention and upkeep, they are reclaimed by the earth, falling victim to the seasons ~ the weeds and the saplings.

Chapter 2

At The Movies

I began my freshman year of high school in the fall of 1963 at Sesser, Illinois. The city of Sesser has in it's town center, an old opera house: *(Figure 6)*.

Figure 6: Sesser Opera House. My first real paying job.

Built in 1914, it first served as an opera house, then a vaudeville house. Later it was a silent movie theater. Today it's a restaurant and presents live shows. It was a movie theater back in 1963 when a friend and I bought tickets to see a second run B-picture and a few cartoons. Before the show started the projectionist came down into the seating; since he knew my friend he stopped to speak with us. He stated he was quitting his job and asked if we knew anyone who might be interested in taking it over. I asked what it paid per hour. "Fifty cents," was his reply.

I told him I would like to take a shot at it. It was not the money which attracted me to the job but rather the simple concept of getting to work in a movie theater with all the perks: free movies, popcorn, and sodas.

He took me and my pal up to the projection booth by way of some narrow spiral steps, which led into a small cramped area, with two large 35mm projectors. The source of light in the projectors were carbon sticks: one negative and one positive. When these two would meet via an electrical tracking device you had light: a great light. So hot, it required a stovepipe to allow the heat out. I won't go into the details of how these projectors worked but the basics are: a reel of film goes through the light source, by way of sprockets and ends up on a take up reel. I took the job, and quickly learned it, however mistakes will happen.

One particular evening I was running the film "Giant" with Rock Hudson and Liz Taylor. I'm sure you have noticed on trips to the movies, those little circle scratches appearing from time to time in the upper right hand corner of the screen. The first one lets the projectionist know: *this* reel of film is about over. Then comes the second circle, and at that exact second the projectionist does some fancy footwork with a special pedal which transfers the operation from one projector to the other. When all goes well the movie is seamless. The viewer is unaware.

On this particular night, after I transferred to the second projector, I looked out at the screen as customary. Everything looked alright. The picture was in frame. The light was bright. It was then I heard a crackling sound. I looked down and was horrified to discover I had failed to attach the film to the take-up reel. All the film, having passed through the gate, was being packed tightly into a small compartment of the projector.

In a panic I shut the projector off, failing to drop the shield to block out the intense light. I looked at the screen again, and in the middle of the giant image of Rock and Liz sharing a tender moment, there was a brown spot, about two feet in diameter. It then spread like a wildfire, which technically is what it was. The heat consumed the entire image on the screen. I dropped the light shield, much to late, and it took the audience less than a second to start with the foot stomping, *"WE WANT A SHOW! WE WANT A SHOW!"*

Since it was known by many who the culprit was up there in the little projection booth, I heard my name called out a couple times, accompanied by a few expletives. This did nothing to relieve my anxiety. The film had been packed in so tightly I had to use a crowbar to pry it loose. It finally spring out like a jack-in-the-box. It took a few minutes to re-thread the film. After all was said and done the section of film I thought was ruined, was later salvaged, minus the one frame which had gone up in flames.

I shall never forget one night when the theater manager had a bright idea to have, on Halloween night, a fright night special. It was a miserable cold rainy night. I ran the coming attractions, five cartoons, and two features; "13 Ghosts" and Alfred Hitchcock's "Psycho." On this night there was one lone kid, Wayne Kirkpatrick, sitting among all those empty seats. Wayne was a guy in my class, who had of his two front teeth, one silver tooth, and he always wore one of those fur hats with the flaps on the sides. I still recall his figure, all alone in the big dark theater, with the hat, seated front and center, illuminated by the reflection from the screen.

At school the next day, I told a friend, Dan Manker, about working all night for the lone customer ~ Wayne Kirkpatrick. Dan topped it off with his unique sense of humor when he leaned over to me and said, "Wayne probably snuck in!"

A Beatle & A Hustler

Some believe the movie "The Hustler," starring Jackie Gleason & Paul Newman, was based on the life of Rudolph Wanderone: *(Figure 7)* AKA "Minnesota Fats." Facts are: Fats was known as New York Fatty, as well as some other monikers. After the movie came out, he started calling himself Minnesota Fats.

Figure 7: Rudolph Wanderone AKA "Minnesota Fats". A legendary hustler.

He was a self promoter, and many say he was better at promoting *himself* than shooting pool. One thing is for certain: he was good for the game of pool. I saw Fats shoot pool a few times at the pool hall in Benton, Illinois.

For a small coal mining town of about 6,000, Benton has quite a history. It's the hometown of one of the world's greatest actors, John Malkovich. His family owns and operates the Benton Evening News.

Beatle George Harrison stayed in Benton for two weeks in the fall of 1963. His sister, Louise Harrison Caldwell, was living there. Her husband was employed by the Old Ben Coal Mine. As a matter of record, George's mother had earlier sent Louise a 45 RPM of a song entitled "From Me To You," by the then unknown group called the Beatle's. Louise had taken it to radio station WFRX in nearby West Frankfort where the DJ gave it a spin: *the first Beatle song played on air in America.*

During George's visit, he and his brother Peter hitchhiked to West Frankfort. The same DJ played a new record by The Beatles entitled "She Loves You." The DJ even interviewed George on the air, as George's brother filmed it all with an 8MM movie camera. The whereabouts of the film is not known.

In February of 1964 the Beatles exploded, and the rest is, as they say: music history. The turntables and soundboard from the WFRX radio station can be seen at the Old Franklin County Jail and Museum in Benton.

On the square in Benton, there was Barton & Collins furniture store. They had a record rack in the back of the store where they sold 45 RPM records and albums. This is where I bought all of my records: even Beatle records. During his stay in Benton, George went to Barton & Collins and bought a record by James Ray called "Got My Mind Set On You." In 1988, George recorded the song. It went to Number One on the charts. George bought his Rickenbacker guitar from Fenton's Music Store in Mt. Vernon, 20 miles north of Benton. The guitar is on display at the Rock & Roll Hall of Fame in Cleveland, Ohio.

Basketball legend Doug Collins grew up right there in the front of the county jail while his father served as the Sheriff of Franklin County.

Benton even had a hanging on April 19, 1928 when a gangster named Charlie Birger: *(Figure 8)* took the big drop, between the jail and city hall with thousands in attendance.

*Figure 8:
Charlie Birger
on the eve of his
execution.*

He had been convicted of plotting and causing the murder of Mayor Joe Adams of West City, a village just west of Benton. My Grandfather was present for the hanging and he, along with all those close enough, heard Charlie utter the words: "It is a beautiful world" mere seconds before Sheriff Jim Pritchard pulled the lever dropping Charlie into eternity: *(Figure 9).*

Figure 9: Charlie Birger mere seconds from hanging. April 19, 1928. Benton, Illinois.

Today you can visit Benton's Old Franklin County Jail Museum and see where Charlie spent his final days, hours, and minutes, as well as the noose he was hanged with. There's even a replica gallows sitting where the original gallows stood.

29

Gangsters and bootlegging have always been popular topics of conversation in and around Franklin County, but when I was growing up around there the big deal was ~ billiards.

Just twelve miles south of Benton lies Johnston City. There, in the rear of a nightclub called Janscos, the greatest pool hustlers of the world would gather. A big ABC Wide World of Sports truck would be parked out back, and the place would be buzzing with activity. So much so, the Department of Justice shut the whole operation down due to the gambling taking place.

This was all exciting, but it was in Benton's pool hall where I first saw Minnesota Fats play the game of pool. Fats lived in Dowell, Illinois, a hamlet located about 20 miles west of Benton. While passing through one winter on his way down south to do some hustling, Fats had a minor vehicle accident and while waiting on repairs to his car he met a young waitress, decided to marry and make Dowell his home. He and his wife lived there with no less than 30 or 40 dogs and cats.

The pool hall in Benton was a classic. It's no longer there, but it was in the first block on North Main. Inside, the place was smoky and dark except for a lone light hanging over each table. The walls were lincd with large framed portraits of the greats in billiards, each decked out in a tuxedo. The tables were all first class slate with leather pockets. When you finished a game, all you had to do was flip a dime on the table and yell, *"RACK'EM."* A boy would rack the balls and off you'd go with another game. Snooker was a popular game there.

One day, the great Minnesota Fats walked in and challenged a local kid to a game of nine ball. There were some kids from Benton years ago who could shoot some serious pool. The game didn't last long, as the local kid called the pocket on the break and then proceeded to run the table. As a reward, Fats took the kid outside and popped open the back of his Country Squire station wagon to reveal a case full of pool cues. These cues were works of art, some with inlaid pearl handles. Fats then said, "pick one kid." You would have thought it was the boy's birthday.

In 1992 while living in Nashville, I ran into Fats at the Stockyard Restaurant. He was living the good life, at the exclusive Hermitage Hotel and of course: he was still hustling. Fats recalled giving the pool cue to the kid. He said, "Hell, I used to give cues away all the time. The manufacturers gave'em to me for endorsements. If I didn't give some away now and then I would've had pool sticks comin' outa my ass."

I saw Fats shortly before his death. It was on I-65, north of Nashville. I was sitting in bumper to bumper traffic. I looked over to my left and there was Fats. I tooted my horn and yelled, "Fats!" He smiled and waved, and I thought, "What a small world."

KXOK 630 AM ~ St. Louis, MO.

Throughout the 1960s, there was a radio station blasting out some of the greatest sounds for more than a hundred miles around St. Louis, Missouri. A fellow named Ted Storz started KXOK, 630AM on the radio dial and launched the unheard of concept of a Top 40 format in radio airplay. The DJs all had distinctive voices: Richard Ward Fatherley, Robert R. Lynn, and Otis Ray to name a few. And of course, the ever popular Johnny Rabbitt, with his sidekick Bruno J. Grunion: *(Figure 10)*.

Figure 10: Don Pietromonaco, AKA the ever popular "Johnny Rabbitt" of KXOK Radio, along with his infamous little trouble making sidekick, Bruno J. Grunion.

It was a time of musical innovation. The Beatles had hit America in early 1964, so the British invasion was well underway, along with the new American artists staking their own claim on the gold mine of the music business.

In the 1960s, the big thing for any 16 year old boy in Missouri or southern Illinois, was to splash on some Jade East cologne and drive around and around while listening to KXOK.

One hot summer day in 1966, my good friend David Hill: *(Figure 11)* and I were cruising in my 1954 Ford listening to KXOK. The DJ announced he was broadcasting remote, from high atop the roof of the downtown St. Louis Famous-Barr Department Store.

Figure 11: My good friend, David Noel Hill, died in Vietnam in March of 1968. He was a good guy with an exceptional sense of humor.

They were inviting people to "Come on down," and bring with them, colored ice to help create a "Rainbow Mountain of Ice." There were free hot dogs and sodas and lots of great music. It sounded like the place to be, so we kicked in a couple dollars each for gas. With gas at 31 cents a gallon we had more than enough petrol to make our way along the 100 plus miles to St. Louis. We were off.

We arrived in record time. The Gateway Arch: *(Figure 12)* strained its 630 foot stainless steel self toward the sky and was quite a sight as we rolled across the Eads Bridge spanning the mighty Mississippi River.

Figure 12: The Gateway Arch. St Louis, Missouri. 1965

The arch had been quite a sight even back when it was under construction. Two huge cranes, one on each leg, climbed a little each week until the two massive machines met like giant praying mantises

34

preparing to do battle. They joined together the two sections, completing the arch, as the last piece was set in place at the apex. Within a month of it's completion, about two months prior to this trip, some character flew an airplane through the arch, prompting a KXOK newsman to remark, "Well, somebody had to do it." All in all, over the years, there have been ten airplanes fly through the arch. With an opening of 630 feet by 630 feet, the stunt isn't so dangerous, however it does keep the Federal Aviation Administration up in arms.

In 1980 a parachutist attempted to land on the top of the arch. He did in fact land, but as his chute collapsed he started sliding down the side of the arch and had to know he was doomed as he slipped past the point of no return. Witnesses claimed he was clawing wildly, until he no longer had contact with the surface of the arch.

His wife was waiting at the base of the arch to photograph this foolhardy act, done in honor of her birthday, and his best friend saw it all from the open cockpit of the jump plane, 2000 feet above. The incident wouldn't occur for another 14 years from the time of our St. Louis adventure.

We soon spotted Famous-Barr, which sat just a block or so from the river. As we looked for a place to park, we tried to spot the "Rainbow Mountain of Ice." From our poor vantage point it was not visible. We entered the store and took the elevator to the top floor. Upon exiting we were ushered into a freight elevator with some others for the remaining ride up to the roof. Some had brought with them, coolers filled with colored ice. When we reached the rooftop, we stepped out onto a black tar roof in the heat of the day. It was much hotter there than it had been down on the street. There were several people milling around, kids like us.

A tattered old tarp had been placed on the roof covering an area of about ten feet by ten feet. Upon this was piled the most ugly and quickly diminishing "Rainbow Mountain of Ice." The various colors contributed thus far, were melting together, resulting in a color somewhere between dark purple and black. This heap of slush stood about three feet high. It tapered out, somewhat resembling more a pile of something unmentionable than a mountain of any sort.

There was a small refreshment setup with free hotdogs and drinks being handed out by a gracious little old lady. Sitting nearby at a table was a KXOK radio personality manning a microphone. Between the records being spun back in the station at Radio Park, this fella was promoting the Famous-Barr Store with the exciting "Rainbow Mountain of Ice" extravaganza.

In listening on the drive over we had let our imaginations run. The DJ had sounded so hip, cool, and fab on the air, but there he was, this 40 something, balding fella with an acne scarred face wearing horn rim glasses. We stayed for a little while longer, to talk to some girls, but soon headed on back to southern Illinois. Overall, it had been an exciting adventure. On the way home we listened to the radio for a while and couldn't help but laugh as the DJ on the Famous-Barr roof began his spiel with, "Hey gang, this is where it's all happening. Famous-Barr downtown. We've got free *hot dogs ~ free drinks & this "Rainbow Mountain of Ice' is just dazzling. YOU'VE GOTTA GET DOWN HERE!!!"*

The small speaker in the dash of my car had lost some of its magic. At age 16, I didn't have a clue as to all of life's little disappointments. I think it's why, as we get older, there's a tendency to not soar so high on expectations, ever aware of those inevitable crash landings.

On The Set of A Movie

One day in late 1966, my friend David and I were on our way to Sparta, Illinois, a town 40 miles west of Valier Patch. The purpose of our visit was to watch a movie being made. The movie was "In The Heat Of The Night," starring Rod Steiger and Sidney Poitier. The film, a murder mystery, is set in Sparta, Mississippi.

Over the years I've heard people claim the film was made in Sparta, Mississippi, but it is not so. Most of the film was shot in Sparta, Illinois. Other locations were the cities of Freeburg, Chester, and Belleville: all in Illinois. The cotton field scenes were filmed in Dyersburg, Tennessee. It seemed the political climate in Mississippi had not been favorable for shooting this story about a black northern police detective, outshining a white backward small town sheriff. The film makers chose Sparta, Illinois for two main reasons: all the signs around town would not have to be changed, and the old train depot had the look they wanted. Besides, Sparta, Mississippi is an unincorporated dot on the map: population about 75.

Having never seen a movie being made before, we were amazed at the amount of trucks, cables, lights, and all the people behind the scenes. When we arrived, they were setting up a scene where Sidney Poitier and Rod Stieger share some dialog and then get into a car.   When shooting began, we were instructed to be silent. This one scene took a couple hours. By the time the crew began sitting up for the next shot we were bored to tears. Months later, when the movie came out, I went to see it. The scene David and I had witnessed being filmed, wasn't even in the movie.

My good friend David Hill died in Vietnam in March of 1968. On the Vietnam Veteran's Memorial Wall, Corporal David N. Hill's name is located on Panel 42E /Line33.

Chapter 3

The Day Santa Claus Died

Santa Claus died one day. It might sound far fetched, but he really did die ~ right before the eyes and in the hearts and minds of many small children who witnessed a horrible accident.

December 9, 1967, was a gloomy Saturday as about 2,000 people gathered at the North Park Shopping Center in Evansville, Indiana to watch "Santa Claus come to town." I was there with a girl I was seeing, along with her kid brother. I had just turned 18 and was a student at Lockyear College of Business: *(Figure 13).*

Figure 13: Lockyear College of Business. Evansville, Indiana. Today it's a parking lot.

Santa would be arriving in a helicopter. The air was filled with excitement as the helicopter showed up from out of a gray sky. We could all see Santa's red and white suit. He was waving to the children below.

While attempting to land, the helicopter's main rotor blade struck some power lines: *(Figure 14)*. It was obvious the pilot had discovered his error and was trying to make a correction. A second later the craft flipped over and crashed within a few feet of us, killing Santa and the pilot. A mournful wail went up from the crowd, especially the young children who were still "believers."

Figure 14: The helicopter had just struck some power lines. A second later it crashed mere feet from us.

Those with small children left immediately. Due to the fear of an explosion from the spilled fuel, the bodies remained in the wreckage for a short time: *(Figure 15)*.

Figure 15: The body of Mr. William Bretz (in Santa suit) can be seen in the wreckage.

When it became safe to retrieve the bodies, several men did so. The bodies lay there on the parking lot, one of them in a Santa Claus suit: *(Figure 16)*. It was a bizarre sight, an image to stay in the minds of many for years to come.

41

The next day, in the Evansville Courier, there was a special article aimed at the small children who either witnessed the catastrophe or had heard about it. It explained how the man who died in the crash wasn't Santa. He was one of Santa's helpers. In the minds of those children though: facts were facts. They had witnessed Santa Claus' death in the mangled wreckage of a helicopter.

Figure 16: The body of Mr. William Bretz lies on the pavement near wreckage.

Paul Harvey, on his noontime radio show, touched on the story. I recall thinking it sad, how the focus on "Santa" dying overshadowed the death of two real men. The pilot was 54 year old William Dorr, and "Santa Claus" was 59 year old William Bretz.

Often times a tragedy is linked with a miracle of sorts. On this fateful morning, Mr. and Mrs. Rudy Stieler, along with their three young daughters; ages 10, 9, and 7, had given Mr. William Bretz (Santa) a ride to Evansville's Dress Memorial Airport, to meet up with pilot William Dorr at the helicopter pad. As president of the North Park Merchants Group, Mr. Stieler was the one who had arranged the "Santa Comes to Town" event. There were two extra seats in the helicopter, and the three young Stieler daughters wanted to accompany Santa Claus to the shopping center.

The three girls began arguing over which two of the three would ride with Santa. Mrs. Stieler told them if they couldn't decide among themselves: no one would go. That was that. The Stielers left the airport and went straight to the North Park Shopping Center to await Santa's arrival. One can't imagine how the Stieler family felt knowing how close they came to losing two of their small daughters.

I spoke with Rudy Stieler in 2008. He shared with me how, not only was Christmas of 1967 a bad time for him: every Christmas since, he is haunted by the accident. Mr. Bretz was his friend and had worked security at the North Park Shopping Center. He had agreed to play Santa as a favor for Mr. Stieler. Another side note of this story concerns the birth mother of Mr. Stieler's daughter's. She had died two years earlier from cancer, at the age of 26. It was the girls' stepmother who had decided they would not take the helicopter ride. Mr. Stieler said his daughters were still dealing with the loss of their mother when the crash happened: *(Figure 17)*.

It was an unhappy Christmas all the way around for many families, and it would be the last time "Santa Claus" would come to Evansville, Indiana by way of a helicopter.

Figure 17: One can almost sense the surreal mood in this newspaper photo. The combination of shock along with a reverence for the deceased made the crowd very subdued.

Chapter 4

The Rednour Family

In February of 1968, I was still living in Evansville, still attending Lockyear College of Business, and I was failing miserably. I had no real interest in accounting. My aspirations, at the time, were what some would consider ~ unrealistic. I had been writing songs for quite a while and wanted to do it professionally. It's where my heart was.

I was sharing a room at the YMCA with a fellow student named Dave Linzy. Dave hailed from the great city of Dycusburg, Kentucky. It was about like the place I came from. Dave once told me the biggest thing to ever happen in Dycusburg was the mill burning down.

I owned a 1965 Chevy Super Sport, and Dave was, as they say, "afoot." One day, he said he needed to go home for the weekend and asked if I'd take him. He'd pay for all the gas and expenses. On Friday, February 9th we took off. We arrived at his folk's home around dinner time and had just sat down, when someone came running up to the back door yelling something about a wreck out on the highway. We jumped into my car and were on the scene in minutes.

Two cars had collided head on. In one car, a 1955 Chevrolet: *(Figure 18)* was a family of five. The Rednour family. Thirty-five year old Everett Rednour: *(Figure 19)* his wife Doris, age 28, along with nine year old Cynthia, seven year old Douglas: *(Figure 20)* and Greg, age 12: *(Figure 21)*.

Another daughter, 11 year old Carol: *(Figure 20),* was not with her family at the time.

Figure 18: Everett Rednour's 1955 Chevrolet. The devastation is obvious in this photo. The steering wheel was shoved up to the headliner.

Figure 19: Mr. Everett Rednour. Thirty-five year old loving father and husband. Spoken of kindly by everyone. Life was just starting to get better when the accident occurred.

Figure 20: 28 year old Mrs. Lois Rednour with three of her four children (Left to Right) Carol, 11, Cindy, 9, and Douglas, 7.

Figure 21: Greg Rednour at age 12. A man of great faith. These days, the Postmaster in Metropolis, Illinois.

The family had been on their way to have dinner with Doris' sister and brother-in-law, Mr. and Mrs. Buck Hamby, in Francis, Kentucky. When the accident occurred they were one half mile from the Hamby's home.

In the other car: *(Figure 22)* there was a drunk 22 year old ~ Dexter Martin. He had been in trouble with the law many times before.

Figure 22: This vehicle was being driven by a drunk 22 year old named Dexter Martin. He had a bad reputation with the local law and the Kentucky Highway Patrol.

According to the police report, the two cars met at the peak of a slight grade on Kentucky Highway 70 near Francis, Kentucky. Martin, driving drunk, on a revoked drivers license, was traveling west, in the wrong lane, at a high rate of speed. The Rednour vehicle was traveling east. The collision occurred in the east bound lane.

Shortly after Dave and I got to the scene, an ambulance arrived. The mother and father and two of the children were immediately taken to the

Caldwell County Hospital in Princeton, Kentucky. The rescue workers knew Dave, so they asked if we could transport the last little girl in my car.

I climbed into the backseat and was handed this broken little angel, 9 year old Cynthia. Blood was everywhere. Dave drove at high speeds on those country roads, as I talked to this child, telling her over and over, "You're going to be alright." And I prayed a lot.

When we arrived at the hospital, emergency personnel were spread out all over the place and working feverishly. At one point, Everett began crying out, "Oh No, No." He then began kicking violently and vomiting old blood. The doctor tending to him, told me to hold Everett's legs down. As I held his legs and the doctors worked, Everett Rednour died.

Lois Rednour had been pronounced dead on arrival. One of the boys, seven year old Douglas, was severely injured. He had been sitting up front between his parents. The other boy, 12 year old Greg, was treated and released. It was a miracle he was not injured more, considering the devastation of the wreck. As a passenger in the back seat, he'd had an advantage at the moment of impact. Greg suffered added trauma in the emergency room, when he was placed in a wheelchair beside a gurney, which held the body of his deceased mother. An unfortunate oversight, caused by the tension and confusion of the whole ordeal.

The little girl Dave and I had brought in, nine year old Cynthia, was transported to Baptist Hospital in Nashville, Tennessee, where doctors performed an emergency operation to relieve pressure on her brain.

Everett and Doris Rednour were laid to rest in the Dycusburg Cemetery on Sunday, February 11th. As Buck Hamby related to me 40 years later, "We left the cemetery and went straight to the hospital to check on Douglas. When we arrived, we were told he had just died." Seven year old Douglas' funeral was on Tuesday the 13th. It had been a terrible week for the family and friends of the Rednours.

Dave and I had gone to the funeral home to pay our respects. It was crowded, and there was a heavy sadness and much weeping. It wasn't an occasion where people gathered to say farewell to an old family member after a long full life. There was no laughter filled visiting going on. Those people were pining the loss of loved ones who had been foolishly taken away, far too soon. The three surviving Rednour children were eventually taken in and raised by family members.

I recently spoke with Greg Rednour. He is today, the Postmaster in Metropolis, Illinois. He told me how his father had gotten a new job as a diesel mechanic, just weeks before the crash. After years of living poor, the family was finally getting ahead. Greg, along with his mom and dad, had accepted Christ the previous year. Over the years, Greg had come to think of it like this, "Mom and Dad and my little brother went on a vacation. Someday I'll go to be with them." An admirable attitude for someone who went through so much. Cynthia lost the use of one arm and has suffered several strokes. The drunk driver, Dexter Martin, came out of the accident with only a broken leg and served very little jail time.

My old friend Dave Linzy passed away from cancer on October 28, 2008. He was a wonderful husband and father ~ A good man.

In 2004, my wife Dorothy and I were shopping for furniture in Lebanon, Tennessee. The salesman, a fellow about my age, explained how he didn't work for the store. He was a liquidator. He traveled around helping businesses close down. He told us, "I'm not even from around here. I'm from Kentucky." I asked, "What part?" He said, " You've never heard of my hometown." I said, "Try me." "Dycusburg," was his reply. "Well," I said, "let me tell you what I know about Dycusburg, Kentucky."

I began telling my story, and when I mentioned the name Dave Linzy, he said he knew the Linzy family well. When I got to the part where "in 1968, on a highway, a family of five," he looked at me as though stunned and said, "the Rednour family!" He knew the whole story.

A Gypsy Farewell

While hanging on with school in Evansville, I was still working on my songwriting. I had lost interest in school, due mainly to the fact I had made a bad choice in which academia to pursue. Also, this was the first time I had been away from home on my own, and I was feeling the freedom. Though I was restricted by school hours and homework, my off time was all mine.

Some nights, friends and I would walk the few blocks to Third and Main Street to have coffee at a little restaurant called "The Farmer's Daughter." Later, we would go out and sit on Main Street and soak up all the excitement in our new lives. The sounds of sirens, seldom heard in a small town, seemed to be ever present, as was the coming and going of an endless parade of cars.

We ended our hanging out on Main Street at night after a YMCA worker warned us of the homosexuals cruising the streets each night. He told us about the older men who were called "chicken hawks." They would prey on young men. From then on, after our coffee, we'd make our way back to the YMCA .

I became friends with a fellow student named Paul Whitney. Our common interest was music. We both played guitar, and he knew a few more chords than me, so I figured I could learn something from him. One day I told him I'd written a couple songs and I wanted to record them. I checked around town and found a recording studio, Giant Records, located in the rear of a funeral home. Both were owned and operated by a fellow named Herb Hatt.

Local legend had it that Herb had taken up with an elderly widow who owned the funeral home, and when she died he got it all. The business, her home, money, the works. Herb was a singer. He was into the type of music performed by Tony Bennett and Frank Sinatra.

The date for our session was set. Paul and I, along with a couple musicians I had hired, were working out the songs intros when I noticed the studio had become crowded with people. The kind of people who just hang around recording studios. These type people still exist today. In no time the session had turned into a party of sorts with a bunch of hippies and/or musicians. I recall two viable people who stood out that day, Ron Dechard and David Hoy: *(Figure 23).*

*Figure 23: David Hoy. Master Magician & Psychic Entertainer. **"A Funny Thing Happened To Me ....Tomorrow!"***

Ron Dechard was a songwriter with Tree Music Publishing in Nashville, Tennessee. David Hoy was a professional magician and psychic entertainer. His catch phrase, printed on all his pictures and business cards, was: "A Funny Thing Happened To Me ~ *Tomorrow*!" David Hoy later helped me meet several people locally. Club owners mostly. During a break, someone from the funeral home came around and told us there was a gypsy funeral going on. They had heard our music through the walls and invited us over. Having never attended a gypsy funeral, we all agreed to go around and check it out.

Upon entering, the first thing to catch my eye was the closed casket sitting on the floor in the middle of the room. Around the casket sat several men playing cards on it. Glasses of beer and wine were lined on the arch of the casket lid. There was a pile of money ~ twenties, fifties, and hundreds ~ in a basket at one end of the casket. This wasn't the pot for the card game. This was the guest of honor's going away stash. I was told how the casket would later be opened and the money placed inside.

Sitting around the parlor, were photos giving a chronological record of the deceased throughout his life. Two gypsy violinists walked about playing a slow unfamiliar melody. Then they would go into an uptempo version of what they had just played. The people, many in number, were laughing, drinking, and dancing. We were given wine, and in an adjoining room there was a feast to partake of.

The men wore expensive silk suits, flashy ties, and pointed toe shoes with Cuban heels. The women, all exotic and darkly beautiful, were dressed in a multitude of colors, and we were exposed to more cleavage than any of our young eyes had dealt with to date.

What with the bad reputation of gypsies, we were all wondering if we were somehow like lambs, about to be fleeced. It was some farewell party. It was still going strong when we left. I heard later, the funeral party went on for three days.

Dropping Out ~ Joining Up

About this time it became obvious to me and my family, I wasn't going to make it in the big wonderful world of accounting. I was in great turmoil. In 1967/68, an awful lot of us were out of sorts. It's one thing to observe life as your living it, (as though with blinders on) from only your perspective. It's another thing altogether to examine the same time frame in a bigger picture. Today I look back and see why I was so confused and without aim or purpose. America was in a helluva mess. The Vietnam war was raging, there was political unrest, drugs were prevalent, and my generation was converging on it all with great abandon. I hung around school for a while longer, then I quit to get a job. One day in late March of

1968 I was walking past the Army Recruiting Station in Evansville. I went in just to check the place out. I had no conscious intention of joining the army, but I also recall feeling desperate and lost, cornered like a rat, looking for a way out to anywhere. An hour later I walked out with a bus ticket to Louisville, Kentucky. I had just joined the United States Army. It seemed like the U.S. Army was a ready made solution to all my problems after all! I had a feeling this was one job I wouldn't or couldn't just walk away from.

I went through boot camp at Fort Knox, Kentucky. Eight weeks of pure hell. From there it was a long bus ride to Fort Gordon, Georgia. Another eight weeks of Military Police training, more intense than boot camp. Then came Vietnam.

I have, burned in my mind, faces of fellas with whom I went through training and served with ~ without a single name to attach to them. In talking with other veterans I have found I'm not exclusive in this. Of the hundreds of guys I knew in the service, the ones whose names I can recall and have stayed in touch with ~ I can count on one hand.

Vietnam

I arrived in Vietnam on December 24, 1968 and departed on December 23, 1969. I had just turned 19. I served my country honorably, as did hundreds of thousands of others. As a Vietnam Veteran, I feel my contribution was minimal.

A lot has been written about the war. There are 58,249 names on the Vietnam Veteran's Memorial Wall; many others came home crippled for life in one way or another.

We were young. Most of us had never been far beyond our home states, when we were sent off to a distant land: foreign in every aspect. We were adventuresome and anxious in the prospects of new experiences. We grew up over there. At that point and time in our lives, we didn't have a choice.

As far as the war is concerned ~ did we succeed? Maybe. Maybe not! History has not been kind to us, and we all came back changed ~ forever! And in the immortal words of Forrest Gump, "That's all I have to say about that."

Chapter 5

Fort Knox

The first thing people think of when they hear the words Fort Knox? Gold! The gold depository: *(Figure 24)* sits right at the edge of the post ~ visible from Kentucky's Dixie Highway.

Figure 24: Fort Knox Gold Depository. Fort Knox, Kentucky

It's located on Department of Treasury property adjacent to the main post, but in reality it sits smack dab on Fort Knox. Fort Knox/Gold Vault. The two names are inseparable.

In 1970/71, Fort Knox was a highly populated army post specializing in armor, with at least 100,000 soldiers in boot camp and various stages of armor training, as well as another several thousand in permanent party. I was of the latter.

Upon returning from Vietnam, I had eighteen months left on my enlistment obligation. On a cold miserable snowy January morning I reported for duty with the 543rd Military Police Co., located on Gold Vault Road. I started out on the wrong foot with the most disagreeable First Sargent a soldier could hope to never have.

I walked into his office and handed him my assignment orders. The orders were in the form of a Western Union telegram, a tell tale sign some political influence had been used to secure my assignment with the 543rd. I had in fact, called upon my Congressman's help in the matter.

About three weeks before leaving Vietnam, I had received orders for Camp Pickett, Virginia. Having never heard of the place, I inquired with the head of personnel. He informed me Camp Pickett was the home of a war college and a federal game reserve. He said I'd be doing nothing more than standing at a gate and saluting all day long. Spit and polish: the last thing I wanted after Vietnam. I had considered police work as my life long vocation, and the army was supposed to provide me with the experience. First, they sent me on the other side of the world, as far removed from police work as possible, and now they were going to zap me off to some high ranking summer camp to stand at a gate and salute all day long. My friend in personnel advised me to write my congressman. I did; I received a letter from Illinois Congressman Kenneth Gray's office advising me to, upon my arrival home, call a Colonel Smith at the pentagon.

I did. The colonel's liaison at the Pentagon asked me where I wanted to go. I told him I wanted to pull "white hat" duty at Fort Knox, Kentucky. He informed me I would be assigned to the 543rd Military Police Company. I would be receiving my new orders by Western Union within a couple hours.

I did, and now here I stood in front of this burr headed lifer First Sargent, and he's eyeballing me like I was something he had just scraped off his shoe. Knowing he was holding in his hands a Western Union telegram: still he asked, "What's this?" It was his little power trip over me. He had made his point, without having to verbally express his views on soldiers who go over the heads of the powers that be. With the stroke of his pen and devious pleasure, he sentenced me to duty as a turnkey at the post stockade, where I would stand 12 hours a day, beside a locked door, in a stale air filled hallway, waiting for some prisoner to yell "TURNKEY!!"

I resolved myself to this drudgery for the next few months. I suffered through. The stockade was a crazy place to spend 12 hours a day. There were a couple prisoners who, at least once a week, we had to turn the fire hose on. We would hold the hose on them until they were beaten down. It was the prescribed method of control. I hated the place. Occasionally, there would be a prisoner shipment to Fort Leavenworth, Kansas. Those would break up the routine.

After about four months, I was called into the stockade commander's office. He told me he was aware of how much I hated my job, and there was a situation where I might fix my problem and help someone else out at the same time.

It seemed there was a fella on patrol duty who was just short of being a conscientious objector. He could no longer take working the road. He was being asked to lie under oath by his fellow MPs to protect them from assault charges. He had been witness to many assaults and several other questionable activities. He said it was challenging his Christian faith.

The biggest reason for getting him off patrol duty was, his own safety. Nobody wanted to be his patrol partner, and he had been warned several times that he could get hurt if he didn't play ball. Asking for a transfer off the road was his way of playing ball. He had a wife and a small child and wasn't about to risk himself for the sake of working the road with a bunch of bully MPs. The swap was made. I felt like a free bird.

The first day on patrol my partner asked me point blank, "If you saw me beat the hell out of somebody, what would you say you saw, if anyone asked?" I had anticipated this, seeing how I was the replacement for their problem boy. Without missing a beat I replied, "You were assaulted and had to use necessary force to subdue the individual." "Good," he replied. At this juncture in my life I was willing to say anything to get what I wanted. As great as it felt to be rid of the stockade job, I still couldn't help but think back on my Christian upbringing. In my heart of hearts, I felt like I had just made a deal with the devil.

Being an MP at Fort Knox was akin to being a Nazi SS officer during WWII. We had way too much power for a bunch of 20 year olds. With our .45 semi-automatic pistols on our right hips and a night stick swinging from our left, we presented quite intimidating figures. With saddled white service caps, we always traveled in pairs. It added to the power trip. Around the MP Company, Second Platoon was jokingly referred to as the "Little Gestapo." We felt the label made our reputation even more fearsome. I soon learned the original quizzing on my first day had its purpose. In no time at all I was getting involved in situations requiring me to lie like a dog.

By virtue of the times, 1970-71, race relations were bad all over America. Fort Knox was no exception. When we were called to a service club, or a company area to break up a fight, it was almost always race related. Drugs were another cause for police action. Needless to say, it was easy to begin hating the ones who were kicking, cursing, and spitting on us, as we wrestled them to the ground and handcuffed them. I soon began to accept the satisfaction in giving a guy one or two whacks up side his head, just to get it out of my system.

Race riots were a common occurrence during this period in the early seventies. At Fort Knox, the Patton Club was the usual site. They could occur at anytime, but without fail ~ always on a payday weekend. It usually began with the club manager calling us to escort some unruly person out. This would escalate into a situation where a drunken mob was determined we weren't going to carry out the request. What should have been a simple task would end up with the canine patrol called in, tear gas, and lots of head banging.

The rest of the night would be taken up with paperwork, reports, and statements. It's where the lying came in. If we hadn't used excessive force, we would have been overrun by the mob. We then had to lie, to cover ourselves against complaints with the Inspector General. It was a vicious cycle to be caught up in. All in all, each time we had to lie, it got easier. In our minds we were justified.

Old Blood & Guts IV

One morning I was standing in the middle of an intersection, directing traffic. Things were running pretty smooth. At one point I was holding up a lane of traffic, allowing the the opposite traffic to move. A car at the front of the stopped lane attempted to turn against my direction. I blew my whistle and pointed my white gloved hand at him. I could tell the driver was steamed. I then proceeded to hold that line of cars, a while longer than normal. I was going to show this guy who was boss. After a great amount of time, I stopped the traffic and gave the other lane the go ahead. An army jeep with a big red placard and two stars drove up. The driver came to a stop. I came to attention and snapped a salute to his passenger, Major General George S. Patton IV: *(Figure 25).*

Figure 25: MG George S. Patton IV. During three tours in Vietnam he was highly decorated, including the Purple Heart. His unit motto was: "Find the bastards ~ Then pile on!"

A tanker, like his father before him, he was at Fort Knox for training exercises. He did not readily return my salute, so I was left hanging out there with my right hand frozen to the side of my head. He began with, "What in the hell was that all about?" I don't remember my reply, but I'm sure I did say something, as I recall my lips were moving. He then released on me, a string of profanities indicating how if he ever saw me pull a stunt like that again, we would both have to be taken to the hospital ~ to have his foot removed from my ass! He then gave me a hint of a smile and returned my salute. His driver pulled away. The rest of the traffic came through the intersection, each driver mouthing silent vulgarities in my direction.

A Railway Strike

One cold wintry morning, about three A.M., my patrol partner, Mickey DuBois and I were called into the station house. It seemed a rail road strike had been called, and three boxcars loaded with ammunition were stranded in Paducah, Kentucky. Mickey and I, along with Mike O'Laughlin, had been chosen to go to Paducah and guard those boxcars. We were given a government credit card, and after drawing out three M-16 automatic rifles and an M-60 machine gun with ammunition for all, we signed out an army van from the motor pool and hit the road. The trip took four hours, and upon our arrival we checked in with the train master, and were given the exact location of the three box cars. We were pleased to discover they sat right across from a Ramada Inn. We had feared we would be stuck out in some deserted train yard, for who knows how long, and this was, remember, during the winter.

The motel clerk looked puzzled when three military policemen walked into her lobby, each packing a .45 pistol, an M-16 automatic rifle, and one of us lugging a M-60 machine gun. When we requested a room on the second floor facing the rail road tracks she still looked puzzled. One would think such a scene would cause anyone to ask "Hey, what's going on here?" But she silently complied with our request.

Without a hitch, we got our room key and carried all the hardware upstairs and got settled in for however long this strike was going to take. What with all our prep time, travel, and checking in, it was now around ten A.M., and we were hungry. We placed all our weaponry and ammo in the room's bathtub, and armed with only our .45 pistols we went downstairs to the restaurant, and had breakfast on the United States government.

Later, we sit up our vigilance. We placed the M-60 by the window and closed the curtains leaving only a small slit to peek out through. Mickey, always the one to suggest the first drink, did just that. He changed into some civilian clothes, and went out to procure something, returning with an ample supply. While I sat looking out through my little peep hole at those three boxcars, my two buddies proceeded to tie one on. Being only a social drinker, at best, I sipped on a bloodymary, and kept lookout.

Around dinner time Mike and Mickey had drank themselves sober. We went downstairs for dinner, and dined on filet mignon with baked potatoes and salad. Uncle Sam was treating us good. Back in the room, we all toasted the three boxcars to which we owed this all expense paid getaway. I then immediately went to sleep. The "boozer brothers" went another round at trying to rid the world of vodka and orange juice, assuring me they would continue the watch.

The next thing I know, Mickey's standing over me saying, "Hey man, wake up, the boxcars are gone!" Mike was hopping around the room trying to get his foot into a pant leg. I jumped up and looked out at those big empty rail road tracks, and my heart sank. In the back of my mind I thought about the impossibility of anyone coming into a train yard with an engine and removing three boxcars of ammunition. The odds of anyone breaking into the boxcars, and stealing the contents in full view of passing traffic, were slim to none, yet in the front of my mind there was the thought: anything was possible. Later, at the train master's office we were informed, the strike was over. Our boxcars were on their way to Fort Knox. We asked for the exact time of the strike ending, as well as the time of the boxcars being moved. We needed it for our report.

As it turned out, the cars had been moved mere moments before Mickey and Mike discovered them missing. We were safe. We returned to Fort Knox and were commended for a job well done.

An Indian Uprising

During my eighteen months at Fort Knox, I saw murder, rape, suicide, and child abuse. All the side effects of alcoholism and drug abuse mixed with domestic violence. But the drinking and fighting wasn't always a serious matter.

I knew two Cherokee Indians stationed at Fort Knox. Their names were Billy White Rabbit and Johnny Thundercloud. Nicest guys you could ever hope to meet, until they started drinking! My first experience with these two was at the post bowling alley. Four MP units had been dispatched regarding a riot. When we got there, it looked like one of those staged fights you see in the movies. White Rabbit and Thundercloud were standing back to back taking on about five other guys, and the other guys were getting the stew beaten out of them. We couldn't get to the Indians, so we started grabbing the losing side, and I think they were glad we did. After things settled down, we asked what had caused all the ruckus. It seemed, during a game of pool, one of the five men had called Thundercloud "Tonto." Johnny politely asked the trouble maker for an apology. The guy responded with, "I'm sorry ~ Pocahontas!" Witnesses agreed, those words had barely left his mouth when Johnny's over sized fist closed it for him. Then the guy and his friends jumped Johnny. That's when Billy joined the fracas. I had a real soft spot in my heart for these two Indians. Maybe it was my one sixteenth Cherokee Indian blood pulling at my heart strings. I was determined Billy and Johnny would not get into trouble over this. I asked the bowling alley manager if there were any damages. He said there were none. My partners took the five "white men with forked tongues" outside and told them they could take off. There would be no charges. A couple of them might have stopped at the hospital on the way.

As time went on, I found these two Indians really did love to fight. If they couldn't find someone to fight, they'd fight each other. I would run into one or the other around post and get a big bear hug. I always gave the Indian sign saying, "Ya At Eeh." I knew it was Navajo, meaning "It is good." It was like speaking French to a Chinaman, but they didn't mind. They knew my intentions were good. They liked me and called me "Brother."

Redneck Lawmen

Each morning around four A.M., a patrol would be dispatched to Louisville to pick up prisoners from the Jefferson County Sheriff's Office. These prisoners were G.I.s who had been arrested for various crimes; like driving while drunk; drug possession; or any one of a dozen other infractions. Many times the individual would be AWOL (Absent Without Leave).

On the return trip to Knox we would stop off in West Point, Kentucky, where a small town jailer, called "Jingles," would be playing wet nurse to three or four G.I.s charged with D.U.I. Many times we would find a couple with knots on their heads from where "Jingles" had laid upon them: his trusty slapjack, which he handily carried in his back pocket.

West Point was a real hot spot for catching G.I.s returning to Fort Knox from Louisville. A lady judge named Stackhouse would hit the violators with hard fines and jail time. After gathering up these fallen comrades, it was our job to return each man to his unit. Then came the punishment handed down by the Army.

The Hit Man

Late one night, my partner and I stopped a speeder. After handing me his license, the driver said he was on his way to the hospital. He turned his head to reveal a bullet hole and much blood behind his left ear. He then took off, leaving me in a cloud of dust and gravel. We followed him to the emergency entrance, and as the doctors and nurses worked on him he gave us the name of his attacker.

With that information we went to the victim's barracks, and with our pistols drawn we entered the sleeping area and turned on the lights. A couple soldiers woke up. I quietly asked one of them where we might find the man in question. He pointed to a bunk several feet down the bay. My partner and I approached the figure who appeared to be sleeping. By now all the men were awake, except this one little Puerto Rican, all snuggled in bed with the blanket pulled up under his chin. I put my .45 pistol to the side of his head, and his eyes opened wide. My partner slowly pulled the blanket away, revealing him to be fully clothed and holding a small handgun. The first words out of his mouth were, "I didn't kill nobody!" I told him, "That was your second mistake dummy!"

It seems the victim had informed on a couple drug dealers in the unit, and they had hired the shooter, the company cook, to kill him. Those two were arrested as well. All three went to prison. The victim survived.

72

Graves and Caves

The main post of Fort Knox, to include housing areas, service buildings, PX, commissary, barracks etc., occupies as much area as a small city, but the entire post covers 105,600 acres: 165 square miles. It consists mostly of tank firing ranges and plain old wilderness.

When the U.S. government decided to establish a military installation there in 1918, the area included some small towns, homes, farms, schools, churches, train depots, businesses, roads, bridges and cemeteries.

The 80 plus cemeteries attest to a time when mountain folks buried their own, right there on the farm. One cemetery contains the grave of Abraham Lincoln's Grandfather. Abraham Lincoln was born in Hardin County, just a few miles southeast of Fort Knox. These cemeteries are maintained by the government through a stipulation made at the time of the purchase.

Small cave entrances are sprinkled over the region. Anyone who has every driven through Kentucky on Interstate 65 knows of the signs advertising various caves. I stumbled upon a cave one day while driving through a secluded area on Fort Knox. My partner and I stopped to take a look. The entrance sat near the road, well hidden by the thick brush. I suggested we come back at the end of our shift and explore it.

By the time our shift ended several other guys had heard about the cave; they wanted to join us. We went to the barracks and changed into our worst clothes, then armed with ropes and flashlights, off we went. My partner Mickey Dubois had invited his brother-in-law to come along. His name was Adrian Gentry.

When the two car loads arrived at the cave entrance, everyone piled out. We began our journey into the darkness standing upright, then after about 75 feet into the mouth of the cave we had to bend a little, and from there on in, it just got smaller.

It was at this point all the guys, except Adrian and me decided to go back: they wanted no part of it. Adrian and I kept going. Finally we were on our knees. The last 100 feet had us crawling on our stomachs in cold muddy water. Creepy crawly creatures were everywhere. Thankfully they were more afraid of us than we were of them.

At last, we came to a large cavernous chamber. It was at least 75 feet across and the ceiling was around 20 feet high. Adrian and I were both so excited to have finally *discovered* this place after the long miserable crawl.

After our eyes became adjusted to the dim lighting, we sat back and marveled in our *disappointment*. Scattered around, were empty beer cans and spent candles. Upon the walls of this place was graffiti proclaiming someone's love for another and of course the inevitable "Kilroy was here!"

Running on the fuel of curiosity and daring, we still thought our trip into that void was torturous.   Now we were crawling back out on what strength we had left and the reality of our folly. Adrian and I couldn't help but laugh at ourselves: The Great Spelunkers!!

When at last we made our exit, the others were waiting at the cars, smoking and bored to tears. We told them about our great discovery. This only confirmed their decisions to stay back, and they were not at all remorseful.

We all piled into the cars and headed to the town of Brandenburg, Kentucky where there exists to this day, the Doe Run Inn. Hidden in a wooded holler, the place is three stories tall with stone walls, two feet thick and massive wood beams. Abraham Lincoln's father, Thomas Lincoln, was one of the stone masons who labored to create what had originally been a grist mill. We had lunch, and then we gathered around the inn's fireplace. Some sat quietly, nearly dozing; the rest of us just talked and took in the rustic atmosphere. It had been a good day.

I didn't get to know Adrian Gentry well and only saw him a few times after that day. Still, crawling a good distance together through muck and mud gave us a common bond. Adrian Gentry was shot and killed about three years later.

Car 1 ~ Man 0

One night, shortly after midnight, as I was riding solo in my patrol car, I was dispatched to a hit and run. This was a routine type call so I eased on out to the given location ~ Wilson Road.

When I arrived, there was one car sitting off to the shoulder by a field of tall weeds. A gentleman about 45 years old was leaning against the passenger door. He was pretty intoxicated. The right front fender of his car was smashed in, as was the windshield. I asked the man for his I.D. He was a Sargent First Class.

I asked him, "Where's the other car Sarge?" He informed me, "There ain't no other car!" I asked him what he had hit. He said, "A man." I took my flashlight and combed the field.

There was a thick fog hanging on the tall weeds. I began my search for whoever ~ whatever. About 50 or so feet into the field I spotted an area where the weeds were flattened. I walked over and found the subject of my search ~ the dead body of a young man. I examined him briefly. He had no pulse. The impact with the car had caused this poor fellow to die instantly, forcing blood from his mouth, nose, ears, and eyes.

Back at my patrol car, I requested an ambulance. The whole time, the Sargent just stood there, leaning and weaving against his car. He was in a state of shock, compounded by the alcoholic stupor. The ambulance came and loaded the body, while I took the Sargent into custody. My first stop with the prisoner was Ireland Army Hospital, to obtain a blood alcohol sample. As it turned out, the victim had also been highly intoxicated. Walking along Wilson Road, on his way home after drinking heavily with friends, he didn't know what hit him.

Later at the station, after all the reports and statements were completed, I was sitting on a railing outside taking a smoke with another MP. A woman drove into the parking lot. It was the Sargent's wife. She got out of her car yelling at us, demanding to know why we were holding her husband. She shouted, "It's because he's black, ain't it. It's because he's black!" I tried to explain, as calmly and gently as I could, but each time she yelled over me, demanding to know why her husband had been arrested. Finally she glared down on me and demanded one last time, "I wanna know right now, what did he do?" I quietly, yet firmly said, "He killed a man!"

She fainted ~ fell to the pavement like an oak tree. I walked back into the station house. I thought, "Let somebody else deal with her now."

Claude, The Likable Hobo

Early one morning, my partner and I picked up an elderly man, nearly 70 years old, hitchhiking through Kentucky without a penny to his name. How he had managed to end up on a military installation I'll never know. He was an interesting character. His name was Claude. We took him to the MP station and placed him in a holding cell. After a while someone had the presence of mind to ask if he was hungry. He was. We sent out for some food, and he ate like a man who had not eaten in days. Then on a full stomach, he lay down on the cold hard steel bunk in the holding cell and went to sleep.

A few hours later, when he awoke, I had the bright idea to take him back to the MP company area and allow him to grab a much needed shower and shave. We also fixed him up with some fresh clothes. During all these goings on he never ceased talking. It was one story after another. He talked of his travels, his adventures and the likes.

He called all of us "sarge" regardless of our rank. During our time with him we found he was a modern day hobo. He said he often strayed from the train tracks and the hobo jungles, still in existence.

These days, we call hobos "the homeless." The urban ones congregate under bridges and in alleys. Some are willing to stay sober for a day or two, to reap the benefits of the mission homes dotted throughout America: a cot, a warm meal, and a little religion. The ones who refuse to compromise must bear the cold winds and poor living conditions. Many suffer from mental illness, growing worse from the malnutrition and absence of proper health care.

Claude was a paradox. Admitting he enjoyed the life he led, he stated he did not particularly respect men like himself. After spending as much time with him as we did, we couldn't help but like the old boy. Several of us decided to pitch in and buy him a bus ticket to wherever he wanted to go. We even gave him a few bucks spending money. My partner and I took Claude to the Greyhound Bus Station on Knox and purchased a ticket for Valdosta, Georgia. He said he had a brother there. He walked up to the bus wearing his newly acquired duds, carrying his old clothes, freshly laundered, in a brown paper bag.

Before stepping onto the bus, Claude turned and yelled to me and my partner "So long sarge, next time I come through I'll bring ya'll some home made moonshine: so good you can smell the boys feet that plowed the corn." We never heard from Claude again.

Shucky Vin Holler, Ky

Life at Fort Knox was never boring. Though it is true, a never ending series of events can become mundane. It's like eating too much of your favorite food. While there were many instances of high adventure, those which stand out most for me are the more amusing simple memories.

There was an old fella from Harlan, Kentucky who would call the MP Station from time to time. He always had the same story. He wanted to report a boy who was AWOL from the Army. He would go on to explain how this boy lived in an area known as "Shucky Vin Holler," right outside of Harlan, Kentucky.

He would then tell how the boy would be easy to capture because, "Once a month, when the family gets their relief check, the boy puts on his army uniform and comes up from the holler to a bar here in Shucky Vin and gets drunk. He then commences to beat the hell outta everybody."

At the time, I couldn't help but be reminded of the "infamous" Ernest T. Bass, from the old "Andy Griffith Show." After a while the calls stopped coming. We all surmised our informant had become a victim of the *wild man* of Shucky Vin Holler."

The Mysterious Harvey Alonzo Buckhart

My partner and I stopped an old junker, which had following behind it, a thick cloud of blue smoke. A fair clue the car was burning as much oil as it was gas. The license plate was expired and the tires on this rattletrap were slick: not a hint of tread. Two men and a woman piled out. The men looked like something right out of "Tobacco Road." They were dirty, with tattered clothes, high water pants and on their feet, with no socks ~ worn out shoes. The female was grimy too. She looked like she hadn't bathed in weeks or years. They were in their middle twenties but looked much older. What teeth remained in their mouths, resembled yellow corn, worn to the nub. If their breathes were a hint of what hell smells like, they would have inspired one to pray daily for sweet salvation.

The girl explained how they'd come to Fort Knox in search of her fiancée ~ one Harvey Alonzo Buckhart. It seems Buckhart had joined the Army to get out of the upcoming nuptials, but she was having none of it. This gal was determined to take Buckhart back home and complete those marriage vowels so, as she put it, "I can get that allotment goin'." She said, "After I get that allotment goin', he can do whatever he wants." The desk clerk, back at the station, checked the alpha roster for a "Buckhart, Harvey Alonzo." He did exist. The trio was given Buckhart's unit address and sent on their way.

Later we were dispatched to a post park. Someone had called to complain about three characters being "unruly and vulgar." When we arrived, we were not surprised to find the "trio," sitting on the hood of their car, drinking warm beer from cans. They were drunk. They had gone to Buckhart's unit, where they were told: he was AWOL. It didn't look like she was gonna "get that allotment goin'" after all. This was not the news she had wanted to hear. We took them to the MP station and made them hang around until they sobered up. Later we escorted them to the boundary of Fort Knox and told them "Don't never, ever, come on this post again."

Love on Hot Wheels

Fort Knox today, like all military installations after 9/11, is a closed post. To enter, one must have proper I.D., and a purpose for being there. When I was there in 1970/71 it was an open post. This made for some interesting police work especially on pay day weekends. When we, on occasions, spotted a motor home parked near a basic training area we just went ahead and assumed it was a house of ill repute on wheels. Sometimes we were surprised to find a legitimate family visiting their son for the weekend, but most always it would be prostitutes plying their trade. At the MP station we had a thick binder loaded with 8x10 black & white glossies of known hookers from Louisville and the surrounding area. We called it "The Cinderella Book." Within it's covers was a mix of young beautiful whores who looked like they could have been Sunday school teachers, along with some real ragged 60 and 70 year olds, ugly and rough by anyone's standards. They all had one thing in common. They were making a living in the worlds oldest profession.

Dealing with the "ladies of the night" required great caution. Many were armed, and many more operated in the company of mean and treacherous male "pimps." When you started messing with the livelihood of these people, it was easy to end up dead. We always approached prostitutes with a backup. When confronted, the girl's would always try to charm us: it never worked. Then they would offer a freebie through flirtatious seduction. When all those strategies failed, they would become out and out, meaner than hell.

Through my involvement with police work, I learned regarding the human condition: you cannot protect people from their own desires or demons (real or imagined). Policemen hold a prominent position on the lists of highest divorce rate, alcoholism, suicide et al. It's because they see the ugly underside of society; the sad elements of domestic spousal abuse, child abuse, and neglect, as well as the plain overall mean spirited nature as it surfaces from within the hearts of others. By the time I left the army I had long abandoned any idea of working in law enforcement as a lifelong career.

Not nearly soon enough my time with the United States Army was up, and I was more than happy to leave Fort Knox. It had been an interesting three years, though it seemed much longer. Just the 18 months at Fort Knox had felt like years.

I was overwhelmed by one nagging question as I was being processed out of the United States Army. It was the same big question mark I had hanging over me the day I walked into the Army Recruiting Station, three years earlier. "What am I going to do with my life?"

I was not yet 22 years old when, on July 28, 1971, I hopped a Greyhound Bus at Knox. As I rode away I swore I would never see the damned place again. Still, I go back often to reflect on the "good times."

Chapter 6

An Old Cowboy

I had been drawn out west by a family friend named Jim McNalley. It was three days after my discharge from the Army, and I had no idea what I wanted to do or where I wanted to settle, so I said yes when the offer was made. I was off to Tucson, Arizona to find a job! Upon my arrival, Jim met me at the airport.

The most awesome sight I saw while in Tucson was on my first day there. Jim stopped off at Davis~Monthan Air Force Base: *(Figure 26)* to see somebody on business. Davis~Monthan AFB is, among other things, a "boneyard" for military aircraft.

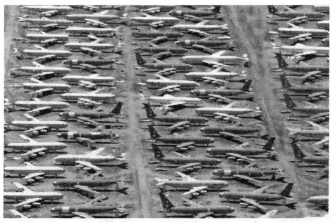

Figure 26: A small fraction of the aircraft at Davis-Monthan AFB, Tucson, Arizona.

Davis-Monthan sits within the city limits of Tucson and has acres of aircraft of all kinds: props, jets, cargo planes, and helicopters, sitting wing tip to wing tip. At last count there were over 4400 aircraft in the "the boneyard." The area was chosen for the dry desert air being favorable for the storage of the airplanes.

Jim McNalley was president of the Arizona chapter of NECA (National Electrical Contractors Association). He was a powerful man in those parts. On my second day there Jim took me out to Tucson Gas & Electric, and he walked into the office of TG&E's president Andy Palina like he owned the place. "Andy," he said, "this boy needs a job." Andy said, "Sure Jim." It was quick and easy.

Jim made me the loan of a pick-up truck, and I went to work the next day as a fuel tender: a job title left over from the old days, though the job itself had long before been reduced to sweeping the floors of the massive buildings where all the pumps and gages were located. One week later Mr. Palina called me into his office, and asked if I'd like to be a "water tender." It was a step up, with more money.

Having not an inkling as to what the job was, I said, "Sure!" A water tender was the person who made the rounds of the plant, checking the PH levels; adding various chemicals to the water, in so many words, treating the water used in cooling the generators used in the making of electricity. I really didn't have a clue as to how it all worked. I just

86

followed the formulas and directions in my handbook. I was aware forces were at work in my favor, and I was having some inner conflict because I was sure, in my heart, I wasn't going to stay in Arizona. Someone told me shortly after I arrived, "You either love Arizona or you hate it." I was pretty sure I hated it.

There were two massive cooling towers I had to climb twice a night to check the fan motors for overheating, and I also had to make a seven mile trip out into the rattlesnake infested dark desert each night, to flush sediment and sand from some large water tanks. On one of my trips out, I came upon a car sitting on the side of the road. The only thing in the area were the tanks I had to flush out. The car was a late model, quite expensive looking. I didn't stop, but drove by slow. I saw no one.

I figured it was some couple having a late night rendezvous. It was none of my business. I continued on to the water tanks. The job of flushing the tanks took about a half hour or so. On my way back to the plant, I passed the car again. This time it was upside down, with the wheels and transmission missing. It really unnerved me to think the ones who had done this had been right there, hidden from my view as I had driven by earlier. The next day I went out and purchased a .38 revolver and kept it in my lunch pail. I had it with me each night when I made the desert run. I liked the job, but I wasn't too sold on Arizona, though Tucson was a beautiful city and the weather was incredible. I didn't know I could breathe through my nose until I had been there for a few days. The city had a beautiful backdrop of mountains, looking like they were but a few miles distant. In reality, they were more like two hundred miles off.

The people were of a different cut. They were friendly enough, but they displayed the same kind of extreme individualism and bravado as the kind of folks who settle in places like Alaska or Oregon. They'll wear you out with the "pioneer spirit" stuff.

I wasn't sure whether I wanted to stay in Tucson. I was reluctant to lay out what was needed to secure an apartment. A 12 month lease, first & last month's rent, security deposit, and a cleaning deposit amounted to a chunk of change even in 1971. Then there were the utilities to be turned on, each requiring a deposit. I decided to take a room temporarily and found one in the newspaper. It sounded right up my alley: $100 a month. I called to get directions and upon my arrival discovered the place to be the Hillcrest Nursing Home, owned & managed by Charles and Katherine Schmid. I soon discovered, they were the parents of Charlie Schmid, the infamous "Pied Piper of Tucson": *(Figure 27)*. I had read the Life Magazine article about him while in high school. In 1965 he had killed 3 girls, just to see how it felt and then buried them in the desert. Charlie was 5' 3" with red hair, which he dyed black.

Figure 27: Serial killer Charlie Schmid AKA " The Pied Piper Of Tucson." His folks were my landlords.

He wore facial make-up, and with an eyebrow pencil he created a beauty mark on his cheek. He stuffed flattened beer cans and rags into his cowboy boots to make himself another 4 inches taller: a whopping five feet, seven inches. In his Cadillac convertible he cruised up and down Tucson's famed Speedway Boulevard, dotted with neon signs from the carhop drive-ins and juke joints. His trial ended with a conviction and a sentence to die in Arizona's gas chamber. In 1971 the United States Supreme Court ruled the death penalty unconstitutional, so Charlie settled in for a term of life in prison. In 1975 Charlie Schmid was beaten, and stabbed by two fellow prisoners. About ten days later, he died. Charlie's parents requested he be buried in the prison cemetery. They never once visited his grave.

Out the back door of the nursing home sat a small cottage. It was surrounded by a hurricane fence, topped with barbed wire. This had been Charlie's house. It was within the walls of this little domicile, Charlie had carried out two of his murders: the Fritz sisters, daughters of a prominent Tucson heart surgeon. Mrs. Schmid had the cottage fenced in because curiosity seekers would occasionally come by and steal pieces of the building: macabre souvenirs.

I was assigned my quarters, which looked a lot like a hospital room, to be shared with an elderly gentleman. He was not at all sociable, but I thought this was probably best as I really didn't want a gabby old man as my roomy. For another twenty-five dollars a month I was allowed to eat one meal a day in the dining room. All in all, I was settling into my new home pretty well. I got along okay with the old folks. I worked nights quite often and slept days. It was convenient, as the old folks were pretty quiet.

One evening as I was walking down the long hallway of the "home," I heard this barely audible, "Psssttt psssttt!" I turned to see this ancient looking gentleman peeking out from his partially opened room door. I walked over and said, "Yes?" His powerful little arm reached out and grabbed my shirt, pulling me into the room. He then quickly closed the door. He started out with, "I need some help with my grip. I'm gettin' the hell outta here." I mumbled something like, "Are you allowed to.....?" "Shsss," was his response, "they might hear us."

I realized I had been drafted into a covert operation, whereby this gentleman was planning to escape from the Hillcrest Nursing Home. I suggested we think the matter through. After talking the subject over for a few moments, he came to realize I wasn't going to just walk away with him and tear out of the parking lot like a couple of bandits. He set aside his grip and said, "Can we go get a cheeseburger?"

I drove us to a drive-in food joint located on Speedway called Johnny's Big Boy, and the old man talked about all sorts of things. Here was a man no one had bothered to listen to in a long time. I listened intently! His name was Jimmy McCready.

Jimmy was 102 years old; healthy as a horse with a sound mind. He entered the world in the year 1869 ~ the year of the completion of the Transcontinental Railroad, when the golden spike was driven: the last spike to complete the massive project ~ four years after the Civil War had ended. He was 31 years old in 1900; in 1949, the year I was born, he had turned 81. Over cheeseburgers and fries and mugs of root beer, I marveled at this living relic who could recount every moment of his long existence in this world. I felt like Jimmy didn't really want to leave Hillcrest. He just needed a friend. After the first day we spent a lot of time together. I would sit for hours listening to him talk of his travels and exploits. He had done a whole lot of living.

Jimmy was born in a gold and silver mining camp known as "Montana Camp," later to be renamed Ruby, in the Arizona Territory. He recalled his mother and father defending their home place against Apache Indians, admitting how a few times the fighting only amounted to his dad firing a couple shots in the air and yelling, "Git!"

A short time later they moved to Tucson, and upon the death of his mother in 1880, the family moved on to Tombstone. Jimmy was 11 years old at the time. Tombstone was going through the transition from an overcrowded mining camp, to a boomtown, consisting mostly of tents and makeshift buildings. The family made a living at doing odd jobs. Jimmy said jobs were in great abundance at the time. In his younger days he had been a bootblack, a miner of silver and gold, as well as copper. He had been a cowboy, and he had even tried his hand as a gambler, but he gave it up because, as he put it, "I just wasn't any good at it!"

He told me Chicago was as far from home as he had ever traveled or had ever wanted to travel again. He and a friend had made their way there in about 1902. Whilst walking down a street they were suddenly ushered into an opium den. They didn't have a clue as to what was going on but went along with their host, a gentleman of the Chinese persuasion. It cost them twenty-five cents each to lie down on a cot and take several puffs from a pipe which had a stem about four feet long. At the other end of the pipe was a Chinaman packing the opium into the bowl and administering the flame. The reason for the long stem was because the opium smoke was extremely hot, and it had to have time to cool down before hitting the lungs. He said when he and his friend left the place they felt like they were walking three feet off the ground. Jimmy admitted it was the first and last time he ever did drugs.

Tombstone is always portrayed in literature and film as a dread of a place where only gunfighters, gamblers, and whores walked the streets. According to Jimmy, Tombstone was like any other small boomtown suffering with growing pains. The place was rough and tough alright, but for the most part it was a town being settled by the working class: miners and merchants. And what today we call cottage industries. It took a lot to make a town spring up out of nothing.

Tombstone's population in 1881 was around 1,000. A short year later, the population was estimated to be 15,000. Quite a boom. With all those people packed into an underdeveloped town, one can only imagine the logistics involved with the housing, feeding, bathing, drinking, and all the other daily goings on.

Then there was the matter of the human waste to contend with, not to mention the horses, cows, pigs, chickens, and ~ well you get the picture. Jimmy explained how most towns back in those days were vile in odor. In those regards, he thought mankind had progressed along very well. I had never thought of western towns in those terms. All I knew was what I had learned from the movies and television. Jimmy explained how he was, on many occasions, exposed to the inner workings of Tombstone's government. At age twelve, he did at times work as a paperboy for the Tombstone Epitaph. His employer was John Clum, the founder and owner of the Tombstone Epitaph. Clum was also the first mayor of Tombstone. This all fascinated me to no end, but what really intrigued me about Jimmy ~ he had known Wyatt Earp: *(Figures 28 & 29).*

Figure 28: This was the Wyatt Earp my old cowboy friend knew in Tombstone, Arizona. 1881.

Figure 29: Wyatt Earp, shortly before his death in Los Angeles, California. 1929

94

Mayor Clum had earlier organized the Law and Justice League. This brought the Earp brothers into the same orbit as the town's cowboy faction.

As an employee of the Epitaph, Jimmy had witnessed many impromptu meetings between Clum and the other town leaders, and it was a toss-up as to who was the bigger headache, the cowboys or the Earps. Then of course, there was Doc Holliday, who stayed aligned with the Earps, always eager to jump into a fray, with or without the authority of a badge. According to Jimmy, Wyatt Earp was an unassuming man. He had a big handlebar mustache, as most men did in those times and a small patch of beard below his bottom lip, which according to Jimmy, usually had a tad bit of tobacco juice in it. Wyatt was more of a door shaker than a high profile marshal, as he is often portrayed.

Wyatt's brother Virgil was the only real official lawman of the brothers. None of the Earps were well thought of. They were considered the type who could straddle the fence between good and bad. They could work as pimps, gamblers, and hustlers and then pin on a badge in some capacity of law enforcement and fight like the devil for good against evil. In regards to being a lawman back in those days, one has to consider this fact: few men even wanted the job.

Jimmy remembered well, the day of Wednesday, October 26, 1881. The date of the famous Shootout at the OK Corral. Jimmy and his father were working near Allen Street. They heard the gunfire ~ something one would hear quite often around town at perhaps three-thirty in the morning, with some drunken cowboy shooting at the moon but not at three-thirty in the afternoon. The incident became earmarked, like the assassination of JFK. People always remember where they were and what they were doing

Word spread fast around town, and in no time the place was abuzz about how the cowboys had more or less bushwhacked the Earps; coming out on the losing end. The gunfight didn't last but about 30 seconds, and there were few witnesses other than the participants, and three of them (the two McLaury brothers and Billy Clanton) were dead.

For the first few days following the shootout, there was much speculation. Then gradually the facts began to come out. It was common knowledge, how for several weeks, tensions had grown strong between the Earps and the cowboys. It was more of a personal thing between the two groups than a matter of official law enforcement. The Earp brothers and Doc Holliday were eventually arrested, tried, and cleared. This only stirred the pot for more trouble and more killing down the road.

The main thing about the Shootout at the OK Corral which puzzled Jimmy and others in later years, was how the shootout gained legendary status and why the location of the shootout was placed at the OK Corral. In reality, it took place in an empty lot beside Fly's photo studio. An alley led back to the OK Corral. Evidently writers of dime novels back east found it more in line with the image of the wild west, if the shootout occurred in a corral. Jimmy said he was surprised how Wyatt Earp and the OK Corral gained legendary status as it began to surface in literature, motion pictures, and eventually television.

Of all the jobs Jimmy had held, being a cowpuncher was, for me, the most exciting. He assured me ~ it was not. Long days, longer nights, endless hours in the saddle, rain or shine, for little pay. It's only consideration: it allowed a young fella the chance to make a living, though meager, while satisfying his wanderlust. He held little regard for rodeo cowboys. He once said, "Hell they ain't cowboys; *they're just athletes!*" He had worked for a while in his late teens as an attendant at an ice skating rink and later worked as a bar-back in Bisbee, Arizona.

Jimmy loved the Arizona sunshine, and we spent as much time outdoors as he wanted. My childhood had prepared me well for times like this. I had all the patience it would take to be this old cowboy's friend. One day he said he wanted to go for a ride out into the desert, so off we went. I was curious as to where this venture would lead us.

As we rolled down the highway, past the cactus and sagebrush; with the occasional roadrunner challenging us to a race, I imagined how there would have been a time when Jimmy covered this same ground on horseback. The highway soon gave way to a blacktop, which eventually turned into a dirt road and a little ways further came to a crossroads. At this crossroads, sat a lone saloon. Two other buildings stood nearby, but they had long been abandoned, near collapsing. Outside the saloon stood a small burro, tied to a hitching post. An old car sat to the side of the place. From the dust on it, I gathered it didn't run or hadn't ran in some time. Had it not been for the old car, I would have sworn we had driven into a time warp.

We entered the saloon. It was obvious the place had been a top-notch establishment in it's day. There were no swinging doors, just an open entryway. There were no barstools. The man behind the bar yelled out, "Jimmy!" Two other men at a table joined in. Those three made up the welcoming committee. They obviously knew Jimmy well and wanted to know what was going on in his life. He told them all about how a great niece had placed him in this prison of a nursing home. He introduced me as his partner.

I suspected not one of them was under 80 years of age, yet Jimmy talked to them like they were kids, and they listened. I had turned 22 just a few days earlier, so you can imagine where I stood with this bunch of desperadoes. My considerably few life experiences paled miserably alongside these old boys. Jimmy had seen the advent of radio, telephone, automobiles, motion pictures, airplanes, and television. A man had even walked on the moon! I recall asking Jimmy how he felt each time these great strides were made. He assured me it all happened so gradually, there was no shock at all. To him, a man walking on the moon was no more far fetched than seeing his first indoor flush toilet. He had known a time when both were unthinkable.

We sat in the saloon, sheltered from the desert heat, drinking shots of whiskey chased with cold beer. The stories my old new friends shared with me would have made great screen plays. They informed me how, right up until the end of World War II, Arizona had remained pretty much unchanged. It still had the "old west" feel to it as late as 1971. It was perpetuated by the aforementioned "pioneer spirit."

Jimmy and I spent the night at the bar. I slept on a couch in the back room while Jimmy slept in a spare bed upstairs. The next morning we both knew something would be said about our outing. Sure enough, Mrs. Schmid gave me down the pike for traipsing off with Jimmy, explaining how she was legally bound for the safe care of the fragile little old gentleman. I promised it would never happen again. As I left her office, I walked past Jimmy. He gave me the insider's wink and said, "partners!" I gave him a "thumbs up!" For the next three months, Jimmy and I were inseparable. When I wasn't at Tucson Gas and Electric, I was with Jimmy.

He swore he couldn't stand to be around old people, which in itself was kind of funny, so we jumped at each opportunity to get away from the nursing home. Jimmy and I made the rounds. One day he accompanied me to The Chicago Store, a three story building literally packed with guitars and violins; any kind of musical instrument one could imagine. I purchased an Epiphone acoustic guitar and was quite fond of the thing. Five years later I pawned it in Nashville, and didn't have the money to get it back. I lost it for the sake of gas money. One night we stopped at a place in Tucson called "Nashville West" and caught a new singer named Tom T. Hall: *(Figure 30)*. He had a single out entitled, *"The Year Clayton Delaney Died."* Jimmy loved the song.

Figure 30: Tom T. Hall.
Singer/Songwriter,
The Story Teller.

We had to keep our running around to a minimum, as Mrs. Schmid kept her evil eye trained on us. One day, we took a ride out to "Old Tucson," a movie set town built in 1939 for the movie "Arizona." It wasn't the touristy kind of place it is today. As we gandered about the makeshift buildings and dirt streets with watering troughs and hitchin' posts, Jimmy chuckled and proclaimed the place was too quiet and clean.

We made one more trip out to the saloon. After a couple beers, Jimmy told his old friends goodbye. This time it was with a sense of finality. In February of 1972 I decided to return to southern Illinois. I said goodbye to my old friend. I thanked him for his friendship and all the good times we'd had together. Jimmy gave me a bone crushing handshake with a big hug, and tears filled his old eyes. I have no idea when Jimmy McCready died. I'm sure he was ready when his time came. He had often talked of Jesus and Heaven. I remember him once saying to me, "Don't this old world make you wanna go home?" He'd certainly had enough time to prepare for the journey.

The Rail Road

When I returned to southern Illinois from Arizona, it didn't take long to find another job. When you're young, there's always a new beginning waiting over the next hill. Those kinds of opportunities begin to wane as the world stops honoring boyish grins and idealistic dreams and schemes. But in 1972, I still had it going for me. I landed feet first in Decatur, Illinois. Once again, someone had gone out on a limb for me and gotten me a job. This time as a switchmen with the Norfolk and Western Rail Road. I have to admit, when I was a child dreaming of what I wanted to be when I grew up, a railroader wasn't on the list. The pay was good, and I could work lots of hours on the extra board.

The first night on the job my foot slipped while I was jumping onto a moving boxcar. I was nearly dragged to death. It almost got me killed and fired in the same night. I hung in there though, and within a week I had the job down pretty good. For the most part it was tedious work: releasing the air from the brakes on a string of boxcars. Then as the engineer kicked the boxcars down the main line, I would throw the proper switches to direct the cars onto whatever number tracks they were assigned.

One of the first things I learned working on the railroad was, "never walk or stand between the rails: only and always between the tracks." A boxcar can travel along a track moving as silent as death.

Once there was a fella, long before I started work there, standing between the rails near the coupling of a boxcar; another boxcar came in and caught him at the waist. He was in shock, but he knew what was happening. He knew he was going to die. He asked for a cigarette and told his boss what to tell his wife and kids. The couplings of the box cars were actually holding him together, giving him time to make his farewell. When he was ready, he gave the foreman the nod, and the engineer pushed one of the cars forward. The foreman pulled the pin. The engineer then backed the engine off, and the poor fella dropped over dead.

I never felt comfortable working for the railroad. The good pay never became a factor in whether or not to stay or go.

One night, I was dropped off at a bend in the tracks and was overcome with a smell I could only identify as "something dead." I was standing next to eight open train cars filled to the brim with parts of butchered cattle: hooves, snouts, ears, tails and what ever else is used in the making of gelatin.

I quit Norfolk & Western, and headed back home. I was 22 years old, and in regards to what I wanted to do with the rest of my life: I was lost.

The New Alcatraz

As I noted before, when you're young it all comes quick and easy. When I returned home from Tucson, I was at a loss for what type of employment I would seek in southern Illinois. The area was so depressed. With proper connections, there was a shot at getting on with the mines. I really had no inclination toward the mines. I had never had a family member work the mines; hence, I really had no connection. Besides, all my life I had seen the devastation of friends losing loved ones in mining accidents. The alternatives were the few small factories located in the area. Borg-Warner had a plant in Herrin, Illinois, where washers and dryers were made. My father had worked there when I was growing up. When I left Decatur I was still in the same situation, now with two strikes against me.

My old high school friend, Dan Manker and I were having a beer at The Italian Club in the town of Coello. Nick Bulla, an old family friend, mentioned they were hiring correctional officers at Marion Federal Prison in nearby Marion. Marion Federal Prison was opened in 1963. It replaced the infamous Alcatraz, which still sits in San Francisco Bay. Like Alcatraz, Marion was where the other federal prisons sent their trouble makers. The next day I went and applied for the job and got it.

After some preliminaries, those of us who had been newly hired were sent to the Atlanta Federal Prison for a two week training seminar. It was pretty intense. One of the things we had to do was interview prisoners, reporting our thoughts on each individual.

If a prisoner can gain your confidence with deceit: next he's got you doing favors or running errands for him or some such nonsense. Once you've compromised your position of authority in the prison system, the prisoner uses it as a thing to hang over your head. On and on it goes until you get caught or just quit to escape the trap you've gotten yourself into. During this assessment exercise there was a fella who looked like a choir boy. He was 25 years old. His name was Bryan. Our panel of four interviewed him. He explained how he had fallen in with the wrong crowd and got involved in a bank robbery. Just by association he was tried and convicted. Most of us gave him a pretty good rating. He seemed sincere. Later in class we discovered we had all been taken for a ride.

In truth, Bryan had been involved in a bank robbery in Florida. He and his partner had taken a husband and wife as hostages. Once they were in the clear they shot the husband outright. Bryan's cohort raped the woman. When he finished with her Bryan decided to take his turn. He then shot her three times in the head, cut out her heart and ate part of it. He completed his act by removing all her bodily organs, and dumping her body down a well.

Once again, I was in a job I knew I would not stay with. Back at Marion, I went to work in one of the cell houses. I found the other correctional officers as difficult to deal with as the convicts. One of the inmates was an elderly Italian man named Paul John Frankie Carbo: *(Figure 31)*. At age 68, Carbo looked like a kindly little old grandfather. He would walk around with a Chicago Tribune tucked under his arm as he listened to ballgames on a transistor radio. The prison had a library with a case file on each prisoner. I made a point to go in one day and pull Carbo's file. It was about eight inches thick. In 1961, Frankie Carbo had been sentenced to 25 years for extortion in the boxing rackets. He was suspected by many, to have been responsible for the drug overdose death of World Heavyweight Boxer Sonny Liston.

Figure 31: John Frankie Carbo. How many people did he kill?

Sentenced to the McNeil Island Prison in Washington State, Carbo made the trip east to Marion in 1963. John Frankie Carbo began his career in crime in the year 1919 at age fifteen. For the reasonable fee of fifty cents, he would take a baseball bat and beat somebody to death. Many times he was charged with murder. When trial time came around, key witnesses would turn up missing or dead. He had played a big role in the infamous Murder Inc: A setup whereby gangs could call in assassins from different cities to conduct "hits." This prevented the police from establishing local profiles. It was widely believed, Carbo was the triggerman in the 1947 killing of Ben "Bugsy" Siegel in the Beverly Hills home of Siegel's girlfriend, Virginia Hill. The file stated Carbo had been responsible for the deaths of at least 500 people.

Once a year a black stretch limo would arrive at the prison with Carbo's attorneys and accountants, along with his wife. They would all gather in the cafeteria, and John Frankie Carbo would sign and initial a mound of paper work for the IRS. He owned a vast amount of real estate in southern Florida, scooped up for peanuts during his heyday.

Carbo was eventually released due to failing health. He died in Florida in 1976. I was really fooled by Frankie Carbo. After reading his file, each time he smiled at me and said, "Hello Gary, how are you today?" ~ I felt like a snake had just crawled over my foot.

I knew I didn't want to stay at Marion Federal Prison until retirement. When I was 23 years young, sixty-five years old seemed a long way off. I quit then and there.

Big Time Promoter

After quiting my job at Marion Federal Prison I had an idea. I've had some pretty crazy ideas in my life, and this one goes back to October of 1972. I thought I would promote a country music show. The concept was simple enough. I would rent a place to put on the show, book the acts, sell tickets, and make money! My first step was to contact some booking agencies in Nashville. In a matter of days I had press kits and artist booking info coming out of my ears. Loretta Lynn was at the peak of her career, so I contacted her agency: United Talent.

Her fee of $7,500 was more than I had to work with, so I took a look at Hank Williams Jr. He wanted $4,500 plus I would've had to provide the sound system, complete with four microphones as well as a piano. I considered it, but decided against it after talking with another promoter who had booked Hank Jr. just a couple years earlier. He said the turnout had been poor, and he had pretty much broke even. Keep in mind, this was three years before Hank Jr.'s fall from a mountain and his eventual rise to superstar status.

My next choice was Waylon Jennings: *(Figure 32)*. Waylon had been around awhile with moderate success. He currently had a song out entitled "Good Hearted Woman." This was before the outlaw craze catapulting Waylon Jennings and Willie Nelson into their phenomenal leap of success. Waylon's fee at the time was $1,500. I booked Waylon, and then for a second act I went with Charlie Louvin: *(Figure 33)* with a fee of $750. I had my date set for Wednesday, October 4, 1972.

Figure 32: Waylon Jennings

Figure 33: Charlie Louvin.

I had my two country music stars and I had my location booked: the enormous West Frankfort High School Auditorium with a seating capacity of 4,500. The fee for the auditorium was a reasonable $100. In my simple inexperienced little mind, I was drowning in delusions of grandeur. I would sell 4500 tickets at $3 each, taking in $13,500. Deducting the artist's fees of $2,250, plus another $1000 for the auditorium, tickets, radio spots, etc., would leave me with $10,250 profit. It was so easy. Hey! Why wasn't everybody doing it? I had placed a

P.O. Box on the radio spots and posters, so there had been some advance ticket sales, though not much. I was thinking the bulk of the crowd would show up on the night of the show.

When the night came, Charlie Louvin and his band arrived and began to set up. I was running around trying to do ten things at once. I even had some family and friends who were kicking in to help. While all this was going on, Waylon Jennings and the Waylors arrived in a ugly old bus: painted flat black and stripped of most of the seats. His band, in contrast to Charlie's, looked like a biker gang. The show finally began; Charlie went on first.

When I had returned the contracts to the talent agencies, I had included half of the performance fees. The balance was to be paid on the night of the show: before the show. Charlie had gone on without collecting the balance of his fee. Waylon's road manager, on the other hand, required the balance of $750 before Waylon would go on stage. I went to the box office and found after all was said and done, I was $20 short of having enough to pay Waylon's balance. My old friend, David Webster, gave me the $20 I needed to pay off Waylon's balance.

All in all, the show was good. But from where I was standing, I was looking at 4,500 seats, in which 4,200 of them were empty. The 300 souls who showed up were all gathered in one little area of the auditorium. It was a pathetic sight.

Fact was, I had lost a lot more than money. For starters, it was my father's money I had lost. I had also lost my elusive dream in which I would do this for a living and make a good living doing it. When I took Waylon's money to his road manager, we climbed onto Waylon's bus. Waylon must have noticed I was a broken spirit. He reached under a seat and pulled out a half empty bottle of Wild Turkey, offering me a drink. I swallowed a couple shots, but a little booze wasn't going to make things any better.

I then went to see Charlie in his bus and told him I didn't have his $375. I looked him right in the eyes and told him I'd get the money to him. He gave me an address where I could mail it and shook my hand, thanking me. He said he could tell I was an honest person. He then gave me some advice, which at this stage was a moot point. Charlie said, "In the future, don't *EVER* book a show on a Wednesday night." The venture had failed miserably, and it was all my doing.

The next day, after sending off Charlie's money, I did something I had vowed I would never do. I re-enlisted in the United States Army.

Twelve years later, in 1984, I was backstage at the Grand Ole Opry in Nashville, and I ran into Charlie Louvin. I asked him if he remembered me. He said, "I sure do, and I got the money, and I really appreciate you not letting me down."

Chapter 7

Garden Of The Pacific

During my second hitch in the Army, I was stationed in Hawaii. The Island of Oahu. Schofield Barracks. Novelist James Jones, who wrote "From Here To Eternity," once said Schofield Barracks was the most beautiful garden spot in the Pacific. It really was. Before going to Hawaii though, I had to spend about four hellish weeks at Fort Leonard Wood, Missouri: what people call *fort lost-in-the-woods, misery.* I have little to say about the place except it was a miserable hell of a mud hole, and the communities around it were made up mostly of strip joints, whorehouses, and adult book stores. If I never pass through there again, it will be too soon.

By the time I arrived in Hawaii, in November of 1972, Schofield Barracks had been around for a long time. Not as old as the pyramids but ancient still. The buildings were created in the Art Deco style of the early 1900s. The focal point of the post were five massive quads. A quad was made up of four, three story buildings forming a square. My unit was located in Quad C. I was stationed with the 25th Infantry Division, 25th Military Police Company. Over the years, when I have mentioned living in Hawaii, people always responded with, "Hawaii? It must have been wonderful."

Well, Hawaii is like anyplace else in the world: it's what you make of it. Take away the ocean and beaches, and what you have left is just another place with people, living and dying. The TV show "Dog~Bounty Hunter" gave a realistic picture of Hawaii ~ once you get a few blocks away from Waikiki Beach.

In some ways, Hawaii was a hardship tour. If you're not born and raised on an island, then living on an island for any extended period can be restricting. For this reason, our commanding officer would encourage, if not outright insist, we take leave back to the mainland at least once a year. Many people suffered from what was referred to as "rock fever." This particular malady would present itself with attitude changes and out and out mean spirited behavior, many times resulting in criminal acts.

The average civilian sees a serviceman as clean cut as a boy scout. In reality, within the ranks of the armed forces, there are the same criminal elements as out in civilian life. There are people who kill, steal, rape, and double deal, as Fort Leavenworth Disciplinary Barracks will attest.

In spite of the negative aspects with serving in Hawaii, there were of course, many more positive ones. At least in the early seventies. I had spent seven days in Hawaii in 1969 on R&R (rest & recuperation) from Vietnam. The main strip along Waikiki had some hotels and a few quaint little shops. Don Ho was singing at Duke Kahanamoku's in the International Market Place, where there was a radio DJ in a tree house at the top of a huge banyan tree.

When I was stationed there in the early 70s, more hotels had popped up. It was crowded, but still had a certain charm. The International Marketplace was still pleasant. It was clean and first class all the way.

When my family and I spent Christmas there in 2003, it had changed greatly, for the worse. Waikiki was blocked from the sun by the new hotels. Stores and restaurants were squeezed into any spare amount of square footage. It was difficult for our family of four to stay together as we walked down the street. The traffic was heavy, the air was most foul, and the beaches were lined with pale white skinned tourists who apparently hadn't seen the sun in quite a while. The International Market Place had been reduced to a third rate flea market. One of the locals told me how the powers that be were planning on cutting down the great banyan tree, so they could build yet another hotel. I would advise anyone planning a trip to Hawaii to stay clear of Oahu. Do yourself a favor, go to Kauai or Maui.

Filet of Fido

While stationed at Schofield Barracks, I lived on post at times, but the open air billets didn't allow for proper living conditions. At night, while one crew was trying to sleep after working all day, another bunch would have the music blaring and the laughter seemed to never stop. I lived off post a few times. It was okay, except for the cost.

For a short while, I lived with a Filipino family whose house sat square in the middle of the Dole pineapple plantation. Right outside my bedroom window, less than twenty feet away, were millions of pineapples. I went to sleep each night with the sweet scent of pineapple wafting through the air. Whenever I was in the mood for one I would just step outside and take my pick. I learned early on to approach pineapples with caution. The first time I ate one right from the field, I cut it open with a pocket knife and gobbled it down posthaste. My mouth, lips, and chin area suffered a terrible case of citric acid burns which required applying calamine lotion for several days.

The husband in this Filipino family was a chef at one of the big hotels downtown. He could take the cheapest cut of meat, and turn it into a culinary delight. One day I returned home from work, and the family had just gotten back from a wedding. There was a huge amount of food sitting in various containers on the table and counters.

They invited me to eat with them. It all looked great. They insisted on me trying a little of everything.

As I was enjoying this feast, a relative of the family asked me, in her broken English, if I liked a particular one of the dishes. She had asked me a couple times, but neither time could I make out what she was saying. My landlady came to the rescue when she saw my frustration. She said, "Gary, my cousin wants to know if you like the dog?" At first thought, I suppose I wanted to believe she was referring to some little household pet: Spot or Rover. Then as I contemplated the succulent portion of meat in which I had been so happily scarfing down: her meaning hit home.

Instantly, this fantastic tasting tender piece of meat began to feel totally foreign in my mouth. The more I chewed it, the bigger it got. During all this, every eye was on me; no one spoke. They were awaiting my reply. I gamely told them how I was enjoying *it*. The word "*it*" almost sticking in my throat, along with "Fido." It took all the strength I could muster to overcome the gag factor. I swallowed whole, taking great gulps of my drink and I discreetly covered the rest of the meat with some lettuce leaves. I must say though, before I knew what I was eating, it was scrumptious.

Burial Detail

One of the duties my unit had the great honor to carry out, was a three month stint of Burial Honor Guard, in the Punchbowl National Cemetery: *(Figure 34).*

Figure 34: The Punchbowl National Cemetery.

The Punchbowl is an inactive volcano. It was used by the ancient Hawaiians to offer human sacrifices to their gods. Following WWII, the United States was at a loss in what to do with their gathered dead, as well as how to honor the huge numbers of those missing in action. The cemetery was open to burials on July 19, 1949, the date on which journalist Ernie Pyle was interred; it was dedicated on September 2, 1949, the fourth anniversary of V-J Day.

117

The cemetery is one of two hallowed resting places in the vast Pacific for the recovered remains of World War II dead, whose next of kin did not request return of the remains to the Continental United States or in fact requested they be buried at Punchbowl. Of the original burials, there included 11,597 identified and 2,079 unidentified World War II dead from the Pacific.

They came from such battle sites as China, Guadalcanal, Burma, Saipan, Guam, Okinawa & Iwo Jima and from prisoner of war camps in Japan. On the front of the tower, which houses the chapel, is a 30-foot female figure, known as Lady Columbia: *(Figure 35),* standing on the symbolized prow of a U.S. Navy Carrier with a laurel branch in her left hand. Engraved below the figure is the poignant sympathy expressed by President Abraham Lincoln, following the Civil War, to a Mrs. Bixby, mother of five sons who died in battle.

"...THE SOLEMN PRIDE THAT MUST BE YOURS TO HAVE LAID SO COSTLY A SACRIFICE UPON THE ALTER OF FREEDOM."

The Punchbowl is now filled to capacity with 33,230 grave sites. Since August 1, 1991, burials have been at the Hawaii State Veterans Cemetery in Kaneohe, Hawaii on the island of Oahu.

118

Figure 35: Lady Columbia watches over the "Acres Of Honor."

We trained for several days before taking over from the outgoing unit. The training was simple but required a lot of time and repetition. Seven of us would march up to an imaginary grave site and on command we would, in unison, raise our M14 rifles and fire three blank rounds each: the three volley salute. Then off from a distance of about 50 feet a bugler played Taps. The next step involved two or three men who would remove the American flag from the casket and fold it properly in a regimented manner: with 13 folds. It was then presented to the next of kin. This all had to be done in a solemn manner.

The 3 volley salute is often referred to as (and confused with) the 21 gun salute, which is only carried out for presidents and high ranking dignitaries. We rehearsed these steps over and over until we could perform each effortlessly, with smooth movements, and uniform synchronization. We could be distracted by nothing.

The day finally came for us to do the job for real. We were dressed in khaki uniforms; with steel chrome finished helmets, white gloves, white web belts, and white boot laces in highly shined black Army issue combat boots. There was an itinerary giving us an approximate time for each burial. We waited in a bus a short distance from the grave site. When the funeral procession entered the Punchbowl Cemetery: we would get into position. As we stood at attention, pallbearers carried the casket to the grave. When the graveside service had ended, we would do what we had been trained to do: render the three volley salute, Taps, folding and presenting the flag. After family and friends had gone, we would retire back to the bus where we would smoke and joke and wait for the next funeral party to arrive.

We averaged two to three funerals per day. Sometimes as many as four or five: seven days a week ~ for three months.

Playing The Enemy

Another detail we carried out involved a mock-up of a prisoner of war (POW) camp, set up in the Kahuku Mountains. Inside an area surrounded by a twelve foot fence; topped with concertina wire, there were crude buildings for the prisoners. We MPs were the enemy in this make believe war. We were given strange looking uniforms to wear, which contrasted greatly with the U.S. Army's olive drab.

We were instructed to treat the POWs roughly. We were to do just about anything short of actually breaking bones; puncturing skin, or killing them. The scene was set. A pole mounted speaker in the center of camp blasted out a scratchy recording about how bad America was, and how these young soldiers were being duped into fighting this war. Making points on how they were morally wrong and why the prisoners should co-operate with the camps interrogators. At the appointed time, down along a path from the thick Kahuku jungle, came a single line of American soldiers. About one hundred of them. Their hands were tied behind their their backs and a long rope ran their length, linking them all together. Each man had a bag over his head. They had originally gathered at a point five miles away; there they were bound and hooded; then force marched through the rough terrain of the Kahuku Mountains, being hit, jabbed and tormented all along the way. When they arrived in the camp, we took over. It was our job to gather identification information and whatever else the interrogators could use to coerce them into co-operating with the enemy.

Once the initial in-processing was complete, the men, still hooded, were marched out to the confinement area. There, one at a time, we untied them and removed the bags from their heads, shoving them into the enclosure. Within the fenced in area, along with the crude building, there was a fifty-five gallon barrel full of water; a small campfire, and some empty cans. They had not eaten for some time. We threw about fifty live chickens over the fence for the prisoners to catch, kill, and eat. It was quite a sight watching a hundred men catching these chickens. They would wring the chicken's necks; dip them into the cans of hot water and pluck the feathers. Then they ripped the chickens open and removed the organs.

The chickens were then cooked in various ways. Some men found makeshift spits and cooked over the fire. Some tore the chickens apart and boiled them in hot water.

The officials studying this training exercise made note of how the men were working together to survive this most real unpleasant experience, right down to having to share those chickens. It was our job, they explained, to create an atmosphere in which their camaraderie could be destroyed, turning the men against each other. The idea was to develop a philosophy of, each man for himself. The theory is as old as warfare itself: divide and conquer. During their fine dining experience we studied the men and determined who were the strongest, and who were the weakest.

When they had finished eating, we called a formation and took five of the men from the confinement area. There, in full view of all their fellow soldiers, we placed each man in a metal wall locker buried in the ground horizontally with the door facing up. We then closed and secured the locker door. About this time these men were beginning to realize: although this was a training maneuver, they were nonetheless dealing with some heady unpleasant stuff.

The men inside the fenced-in area would call out words of encouragement to those buried in the containers ~ calling us every name in the book for what we were doing. All the while, the loud speaker was still blasting out condemnation upon America and all it stood for. Several of us talked among ourselves and made note of how everything being said over the loud speaker had a ring of truth to it. Another ploy of the enemy: don't try to sway an American soldier with blatant untruths. Instead, drive home the things he knows are true. There are American citizens who will spit on you if and when you get back home. The draft dodgers curse you as they burn their draft cards. The politicians are corrupt, the capitalists are getting rich at the cost of your buddies' lives. For the most part: all truthful statements. The broadcast went on, day and night.

One by one, we would take a prisoner to a place in the compound where he would be subjected to interrogation. All they wanted the soldier to do was give up some small bit of information concerning his unit's location, strengths, and movement strategies. The training lasted three days per cycle. Each day, more harassment, more mental anguish ~ and more live chickens. When the exercise was over, the prisoners were loaded onto trucks and taken somewhere for deprogramming. As for us, the enemy, we started it all over again as down through the thick Kahuku Mountains came a hundred more prisoners. We were on this detail for six weeks; seven days a week. When it was over we went back to white hat duty at Schofield.

One day I ran into a fella who had gone through the POW training. He was a First

Lieutenant who had gotten the deluxe treatment from us. He walked up to me and said, "I know you from somewhere!" I recognized him and said, "the POW camp!" We talked for awhile and had a few laughs. We touched on how the experience had been a strange one, making mention of the after effects from the loud speaker blasting out pure propaganda, day and night. We agreed: the stuff really does work.

Aloha From Hawaii

I was never a big Elvis fan. I was too young when he first spring forth on the scene, though I do recall seeing him on The Milton Berle Show. By the time I had reached my teenage years, the Beatles had invaded America and Elvis was making those awful movies, and of course the terrible record albums accompanying each film. Still, Elvis was much more than a mere singer and actor. He was a phenomenon.

So it only made sense when, in January of 1973, some friends invited me to go with them to see Elvis perform live in his famous "Aloha From Hawaii" concert. Elvis made a grand entry in a helicopter: *(Figure 36)* onto Waikiki Beach. We attended the madcap scene and the crowd was immense. The effect was just as Tom Parker, Elvis' manager, had designed: great publicity for an event to be broadcast around the world from the Honolulu Convention Center. The price of admission to this historical show was: food. Because the concert was being broadcast, the Federal Communications Commission didn't allow ticket sales. Large containers were placed at each entrance. The food went to feed the poor. We deposited our canned goods and took our seats.

It was sometime after midnight; the Honolulu Convention Center was packed. We were in the nosebleed section. The sound system was state of the art; I could hear Elvis just fine, but from where I was sitting, he was about the size of an ant. A young couple seated near us was kind enough to

Figure 36: This was on the occasion of Elvis' landmark, "Aloha From Hawaii" concert. 1973.

loan me their binoculars. I do recall Elvis introducing Jack Lord who was in the audience. Jack Lord, at the time, was star of the hit TV series

Hawaii Five-O.

Elvis put on a great show; it was being broadcast by satellite~live around the world. History in the making. It had never been done before. There was a lot going on behind the scenes concerning this historic concert. For starters, there were a couple taped rehearsals. Many people who witnessed those rehearsals said Elvis was less nervous than in the final live show. Years later when I watched a DVD of the whole show, I could tell there had been a lot of editing and manipulation done to put together the perfect package.

Of course, this was not the first time Elvis had given a concert in Hawaii. Many people don't know this, but Elvis' interest in helping build the "USS Arizona Memorial" in Pearl Harbor, got the ball rolling on the massive project.

After December 7, 1941, the U.S. scrapped and salvaged as much of the sunken battleship, USS Arizona as they could, leaving one of the gun turrets protruding from the water. They just wanted to forget the whole thing, but annual services honoring the 1,102 men still down inside the ship forced the powers that be to agree: a memorial of some kind should be set up.

The U.S. Government said, "Fine, but we're not paying for it. It must be done with privately raised funds." The idea was slow going at first, until Elvis held a concert at Pearl Harbor in March of 1961, raising $64,000. The gesture must have inspired a few and surely shamed a few more, because in no time at all, the half million dollar project was fully funded and The USS Arizona Memorial was dedicated on Memorial Day in 1962.

Jack Lord

I met Jack Lord: *(Figure 37)* at one of his art shows in Honolulu. He was a talented painter and in my opinion a kind and gracious fellow.

Figure 37: Jack Lord. Actor and Philanthropist. Misunderstood.

In 1962, he had starred in a TV show "Stoney Burke" about a rodeo cowboy. Warren Oates played his sidekick who was always getting himself into trouble. I have, over the years, read where Jack Lord was an ego maniac; a taskmaster on the set of Hawaii Five-O. Maybe he was a perfectionist, but I would think it comes with the territory when putting together a show of such high caliber. It was common to see a production crew at any given time on Oahu, filming Hawaii Five-O. The interiors for the show were filmed at Fort Ruger, an abandoned military post near Diamond Head. Some friends of mine would occasionally get work as extras on the show. While they, most often, ended up on the cutting room floor, or they were unrecognizable when the show was broadcast, they assured me the money was good.

While in Hawaii, I met people who had worked with Mr. Lord; they had nothing but glowing things to say about him. For several years he was the Grand Marshal in the Honolulu Christmas Parade, riding a white horse down Kalakaua Avenue. The crowds loved it. When I met him at his art show, he was open and approachable and gave me a few minutes of his time to talk about painting.

Before Jack Lord died in 1998 he had arranged for his fortune of 40 million dollars to be shared by various charities in Hawaii. This was done upon the death of his wife in 2006.

Rick Nelson

I always thought of Rick Nelson: *(Figure 38)* as a regular kind of guy, as well as a top notch performer. I suppose it was from watching him on our little black and white TV for so many years.

Figure 38: Rick Nelson. A regular guy.

When he came to Schofield Barracks to perform, I was lucky enough to hang out backstage and visit with him for a few hours. It was at the Conroy

Bowl, a circular structure built back in the 1930s when concrete was cheap and labor was free. In earlier years the 25th Division had used the Bowl for Unit Boxing matches. In 1974, it was being used for training classes and music concerts.

Rick Nelson had just recently gone through the awful experience at Madison Square Garden where the fans booed him off the stage for not singing the songs he was known for. He was trying to grow as a performer and all they wanted to hear was, "Hello Mary Lou," "Travelin' Man," and all the rest of his hits. He had gone away humiliated, but he sat down and wrote a song about the experience. It was called "Garden Party." It was his biggest hit to date.

At this particular concert, the place was packed. He put on a great show with his Stone Canyon Band, and the crowd loved him. There were ladies there who were from his era and with them were their daughters. Backstage, before and after his performance, a lot of people were coming and going. Rick was laid back and although he was a quiet person, he was friendly and went out of his way to make visitors feel welcomed.

He answered a lot of silly questions from fans lucky enough to get backstage, and he gave interviews to a couple publications. He made each one feel like they were the most important person at the moment.

Chapter 8

Mr. Lindbergh, I Presume

My meeting Charles A. Lindbergh: *(Figures 39 & 40)* doesn't come up in conversation often. He is one of the greatest figures in America's history. Our meeting came about through a series of incidents.

Figure 39: Charles A. Lindbergh with the "Spirit of St. Louis. 1927

Figure 40: Charles A. Lindbergh shortly before his death. Maui, Hawaii. 1974

While on MP patrol one night in late 1973, a friend named Les made a traffic stop on a DUI. Not only was the driver drunk but he was in the company of the wife of a Major in the U.S. Army. It seems her hubby was out on maneuvers, and she was having a girl's night out. The gentleman begged Les to cut him some slack, and after some real soul searching Les decided to let them go on one condition: the woman, who wasn't drunk, had to do the driving.

The guy was so happy to be let off the hook he gave Les a business card. It seems he was the manager of one of the swanky hotels on Waikiki. He invited Les to come down one evening and be his guest for dinner. Les didn't waste anytime doing so. He and his wife found a baby sitter, and down to Waikiki they headed.

Upon their arrival, they were treated like honored guests and enjoyed the finest meal they'd had in a long while. The manager came over later and sat down. During their conversation Les got bold and asked about a part time job, working security at the hotel. The manager said if he wanted it, the job was his.

Well, in no time Les was in high cotton. He was making more money working for the hotel part time, than he was getting as a Private First Class in Uncle Sam's army. The job even included a complimentary room whenever he wanted.

They say good things never last. One evening as Les was making his rounds, a local hoodlum grabbed a guest's purse, and while chasing the rascal on the grounds Les took a serious spill on some concrete. He busted his knee up pretty bad. An ambulance took him to Queens Medical Center. Les was admitted and treated with a cast and several stitches. I went down the next day to visit him and upon my leaving the hospital, I noticed a small crowd gathered around an elderly couple. I asked an orderly what was going on. He said it was Mr. and Mrs. Charles Lindbergh. Lindbergh was being treated for lymphoma.

I wasn't about to let an opportunity to meet Charles Lindbergh slide by. I made a beeline for them. I walked right up like I was supposed to be there, held out my hand and said, "Mr. Lindbergh, it's an honor to meet you sir." He shook my hand and nodded, saying, "Thank You." I couldn't help but think about all the many people this man had shaken hands with. I felt as though by shaking hands with this great historic figure, I had transcended time. I had shaken the hand, which had held the yoke of the "Spirit Of St. Louis."

After meeting Charles Lindbergh I began to search in earnest for information on him. All I knew of him were the basic school book teachings ~ the nonstop solo flight from New York to Paris. I was surprised to find he had, at various times, been the center of much controversy.

In 1938, at a time when the Nazis were ravaging Europe and threatening England, he had visited Germany and was awarded Germany's Service Cross Of The Eagle by Hermann Goering, Hitler's right hand man. This angered President Franklin Delano Roosevelt to no end. Lindbergh later got into more hot water with his seemingly anti-semitic speeches. He had also made quite a name for himself with his attitudes on racial superiority. Although he served his country well and made great strides in the field of aviation, he was nonetheless ostracized by many in America's hierarchy. All of this, along with the much publicized kidnapping and death of his first born, Charles A. Lindbergh Jr., led him to live a fairly reclusive lifestyle, first in France and then in a modest home on the island of Maui, Hawaii.

On August 26th 1974, Lindbergh passed away. He is buried in a church yard on the island of Maui.

Johnston Atoll

Shortly after my arrival to Schofield Barracks, the Company XO called me to the orderly room and informed me I was to be stationed TDY (temporary duty) on Johnston Atoll: *(Figure 41)* for 90 days.

Figure 41: Johnston Atoll. A flat piece of coral 717 miles southwest from Honolulu.

135

It seemed I was the only enlisted man in the company with a Top Secret Crypto security clearance: a relic from my Vietnam tour. I had never heard of Johnston Atoll; the only thing I was thinking about was the $25 per day, extra pay I would be receiving. I packed my things and, the next morning I flew out from Wheeler Air Field. Johnston Atoll is 717 miles Southwest from Oahu.

The Atoll is one half mile wide by two miles long. I spent 90 days there and when the time came to leave, I wanted to stay more than anything. There were about 600 men on JA: two hundred Army and nearly 400 civilian workers. The civilians were primarily engineers who kept the electric plant and water purification plant going.

Then there were the guys who worked the mess hall. Best meals ever served under the guise of military food. They had rib eye steaks; cooked any way you wanted and lobster. The food would rival a five star restaurant. We had an Olympic size swimming pool: *(Figure 42)* an outdoor theater with first run movies: *(Figure 43)* a two lane bowling alley. In the small Post Exchange, cigarettes were only 12 cents a pack. In the bar, a beer was a dime and mixed drinks were a quarter.

Figure 42: Olympic size pool on JA.

Figure 43: Watching movies with a tropical breeze.

By now, you might be wondering what we were doing on this speck in the middle of the Pacific ocean. Chemicals. Nerve gas. Agent Orange: *(Figure 44)*. During an operation called "Red Hat" every kind of chemical, gas, and explosive was moved from Okinawa, Japan to Johnston Atoll. Chemicals used in previous wars were stored there in row after row of concrete bunkers.

Figure 44: These barrels of agent orange represent a small portion of chemicals of warfare stored on JA.

Each morning a team of two (an MP and a chemical worker) would make the rounds inspecting the bunkers. There were two locks on each bunker. The MP had a key to one, while the chemical man had the key to the second. We would open the door and look in on a cage where there lived (or not) a rabbit. If the rabbit was alive we would merely replenish it's food and water and move on, but if it was dead we would close the door. A dead rabbit meant a chemical leak. We would call in a containment team to locate the leak and seal it. Meanwhile, my associate and I would move on to the next bunker. There was a guy on JA who did nothing but breed rabbits, as if they needed any help.

During the evenings, we took advantage of the shark infested waters. We fished off the dock at a point called the "shit chute." It was where the mess hall dumped their scraps. Fish swam around by the thousands. We would snag these fish (most were a foot in length) and then put them on a large hook for the sharks. One time, we stopped at the dispensary and got a pint of blood with which we soaked a rag and tied it around the hook. The blood sent out a message like a dinner bell to the sharks: *(Figure 45).*

Figure 45: We caught 7 & 8 footers like these every night.

We used empty five gallon jugs as corks. A deep sea fishing rod and reel would let the cork travel out until a shark would strike, and the battle began. It sometimes took up to two hours, or more and an aching back, but when the shark was finally in the shallows, someone would wade out with a gaff hook and bring him onto the beach. These sharks averaged seven to eight feet and it took only a solid blow to its snout with a ten pound sledge to stun it. We would then cut it open. The meat went to the

139

mess hall and served for some fine eating. A civilian fella would take the dorsal fins, jaws, and eyes and sell them to a friend in Honolulu, who in turn mounted them and sold them to the tourists. It was here I was shown how a shark's eyeball could be used as a magnifying glass.

Each Thursday a plane would land and drop off people, mail, and supplies. Outgoing passengers and mail waited to go on board. In no time the plane was taking off again. Once a month, a USO show would arrive: *(Figure 46)*.

Figure 46: A USO Troupe arrived once a month. For one week it was great music and beautiful girls.

This was the only time women were allowed on JA. In todays atmosphere, where we are all expected to be politically correct, I'm sure there would be an ample amount of women there, but this was 1973. The shows were always great and the girls always beautiful. Of course, they were stranded on this rock until the following Thursday so it made for some interesting courtships, even if short term.

By the time my 90 days were up, I had grown quite fond of Johnston Atoll. I requested a transfer to JA but was refused. When I returned to Schofield Barracks, I enjoyed the extra money my TDY provided but after the solitude of Johnston Atoll, Schofield seemed like a buzzing beehive.

I went online in 2007 and viewed some pictures of Johnston Atoll. The photos showed bulldozers tearing down all the buildings. It was a shock to see those places being destroyed. A view of Johnston Atoll on Google Earth reveals a bleak and barren strip of coral with a closed runway.

A Tornado At Sea

Several friends and I chartered a boat for a day of deep sea fishing. At twenty-five dollars each, it didn't break any of us. We loaded up the boat one beautiful sunny morning, and set out for open water. Soon we were far beyond the view of Oahu.

The only experience I had with this type of fishing was the shark fishing I had done on Johnston Atoll. It was a little different on the boat, as most of what we were catching were smaller, busier fish. They would turn on a dime, go under the boat and with five of us aboard it got to be quite a hassle. We caught a couple sea turtles and a few hammerhead sharks ~ throwing them all back. We we're hoping to get some swordfish. Our Captain took us to

141

areas where swordfish were known to gather but no luck. Let's face it though, we're talking about the Pacific Ocean, a lot of water, and as one punster put it, "Yeah, and that's just the top of it."

In the afternoon, the water began to get a little choppy and the waves started to get larger. Being in a 54 foot boat in the middle of the ocean, miles from land, you realize just how small and puny you are in the grand scheme of things. With each wave it seemed our vessel went down 20 or 30 feet with a wall of water towering above us: a frightening sight. Then we would spring back up and ride the crest, then down again.

A couple of the guys got a bad case of sea sickness and made the experience, for the rest of us, pretty unpleasant. I was one of the lucky ones. We had brought a lot of food along and several bottles of spirits to drink, but with stomachs heaving, no one had the desire for it.

The sky didn't grow dark and the winds never got much stronger than usual, so we were all stunned when the Captain suddenly pointed out across the water and reported a waterspout. We all stood frozen as we witnessed this gigantic white tornado making it's way across the ocean's surface; reaching thousands of feet into the clouds. This monster was a scary sight, but the Captain assured us it was miles away and we were in "little or no danger." It was the "little" part commanding our attention. He got on the radio and reported it to the

Coast Guard. We watched it for quite a while until finally, to the relief of us all, it just disappeared as though turning into a mist. The water immediately, became calm and the rest of the day was without incident, including, unfortunately, our fishing. Our catch got a reprieve mainly because we were ashamed to let anyone see what a pitiful outing we'd had.

When a charter comes into the dock, folks will gather around to see what it brought in. It's a lot simpler to just tell them you caught some whoppers but only for sport: not for keeps. Later in the evening, we did consume our beverages, and after all was said and done, some of us did get sick, and we all had great stories to tell about the ones that got away.

The Hurricane

In 1974, I was living in a cottage at a place called Mokuleia Beach Colony. It was right on the ocean off Farrington Highway. Dillingham Airfield, where I took soaring lessons, was right down the road. Mokuleia Beach Colony was a beautiful collection of small cottages with immaculate lawn and landscaping. A short walk down a stone path lined with flowers led to the beach. One morning, I arrived home after working a 12 hour night shift. I had been skipping sleep for several days and, it had finally caught up with me. It was one of those times when you don't even remember your head touching the pillow.

I slept for nearly 20 hours. When I awoke, I stepped outside to find the grounds a mess with deposits of sand in the grass along with chunks of bark and sea weed. The pool was filthy. I walked down to the beach and found several homes along the water had been completely destroyed. Some were no longer there. There was debris scattered about.

I went to the managers office and asked what had happened. He looked at me like I had just arrived from another planet. He told me how a hurricane had come through, and just about carried us all away. He couldn't believe how during it all, I had been sound asleep in my cottage.

In 2003, I took my family to Hawaii for Christmas and we made a special trip out to Mokuleia Beach Colony. The place had not changed at all in 30 years. It was as beautiful as ever. During our visit there, we stopped off at the glider school where I had taken soaring lessons. My wife Dorothy and our daughter, Christen, took a glider ride in the same glider I had trained in: a Switzer 2-32. The owner of the glider service, a guy named Bill, was still there and as we were talking I reminded him of the first time we met. After my first glider lesson, I helped push the glider back onto the side of the runway. We then covered it up to protect it from the ocean air. Bill gave me a ride back to my car. As we were driving to the other end of the runway, Bill reached into a music case and took out something I had never seen before; a cassette tape. Until then, in automobiles, people listened to eight track tapes. Bill was now telling me how this little tape was going to be the rage. I looked at it carefully and stated how it didn't seem possible a tape so narrow could sound good. He slipped it into a tape player mounted under the dash and from the speakers came the most beautiful sounds of the group Bread performing "It Don't Matter To Me." I couldn't believe the quality of the sound. Today, compact discs and all the other new technology have made those cassettes obsolete.

A Visiting Prince

In 1974, Prince Charles of England: *(Figure 47)* was serving in the Royal Navy of (his Mum) Her Royal Highness, Queen Elizabeth.

About a hundred feet out my front door was the Mokuleia Polo Field and living a couple cottages down from me were four beautiful lady school teachers from England.

I had gotten to know the English ladies and had dated one of them a few times. We were sitting out by the pool one evening having drinks, when one of them mentioned having seen on the news:

Prince Charles' ship was docked at Pearl Harbor and he had been invited to play polo the next day: right next door.

Figure 47: Prince Charles of England (L) takes a break from playing polo at the Mokuleia Polo Field across from my beach cottage. 1974.

The ladies were beside themselves about their Prince being in such close proximity. The rest of the evening was spent listening to them confer with each other on what to wear; what to wear!

The next day, found us at the match, sitting on the fence, like birds on a telephone wire. I was cheering the players on as if I really knew anything at all about polo. Prince Charles was there and the girls were there and much to their chagrin, so were a great many other beautiful young ladies. I came to understand this was quite an occasion. In Jolly Old England, the closest these ladies could have gotten to his Royal Highness would have been a peek at him in a motorcade.

146

The match proceeded on, and at one point, during a break in the competition, Charles came riding over to where we were. It was obvious his attention had been gained by the ladies. When he learned they were his subjects, the Prince really let his charm flow. The ladies hopped off the fence and showed their respect to Charles with an exaggerated (by American standards) curtsy. Another American "bloke" and I stepped out and extended our hands. I shook his hand with an all American, "pleased to meet ya! how ya doin'?" He responded with "quite well thank you."

Then with all the sincerity of a rock, I asked if he was enjoying the islands. People always refer to Hawaii as the Islands, even if they're talking about only one island. No sooner had the words passed my lips, than I realized by asking this I was implying, if he weren't enjoying the islands, I could do something to remedy the situation. His reply was as mechanical and insincere as my inquiry had been. He smiled and said, "Yes, very much, thank you." He dismounted and stayed with us for several minutes making small talk and doing an awful lot of flirting with my English friends. I found Prince Charles to be quite a regular guy. When it was time to continue on with the game he took his leave as gallantly as he had arrived; with a flair. He mounted his polo pony and off he went. Later, after the polo match had ended, and the Prince was long gone, the girls were still going on about their meeting Prince

Charles. Finally, one of them asked me what I thought of the Prince. I turned to them and said, "Sure, he's well bred and cultured, with the finest education; he's one of the richest men in the world, and someday he'll be King of England, but take it all away and what do you have left?" The girls looked puzzled, and asked "What *do* you have left?" "Me!", I replied. They all laughed and one gave me a big hug and said, "That's what we like about you American blokes ~ your sense of humor!"

The Earthquake

Sometime in 1973, a great portion of the 25th Infantry Division went to the Big Island for maneuvers. The 25th Division was 50,000 strong by this time. We were placed on red alert, and when the time came we made our way over to Wheeler Airfield, which was located across the highway from Schofield. Once on Wheeler, we drove our trucks and jeeps into the bellies of C-130 transport planes. We then strapped in our cargo as well as ourselves. This was quite an operation with the transporting of some 15,000 troops along with the armor, trucks, and jeeps for their use. When you consider the tents and mess facilities, etc., it's really amazing how this could all be pulled off in a matter of hours. Anyone who has any doubts about the men and women in our Armed Forces being capable of doing their jobs to the max, need only take part in one of these maneuvers.

It wasn't a long flight to the Big Island, but it took it's toll on me. I had been feeling feverish for a couple days, and by the time we arrived I was diagnosed by a medic as having a severe case of pneumonia. I was taken to the small makeshift camp hospital and set up with an I.V. and antibiotics. There, totally wasted and feverish; under strong medication, I faded into a deep sleep.

When I awoke the next day, the first thing I noticed were the light fixtures missing from the ceiling. An earthquake measuring 4.6 on the Richter scale had nearly destroyed the place. A nurse told me how the place was crashing around them, with lights flickering off and on. People screaming and grabbing for something to hold on to as my bed rolled smoothly across the room, I.V. crashing to the floor. All this, as I slept like a baby.

A Volcano

After recovering from my bout with pneumonia, I went back to my unit and started to work. With training in the military, one is always shooting for perfection. Leaders are constantly trying to better their troops and shine in the eyes of command. We worked 12 and 14 hour days and when we had a day off, we took advantage of it. One day, a bunch of us hiked down into the mouth of the Halemau'ma'u volcano. It was mostly inactive at the time.

We walked around on the ash and crust, among the spouts located throughout   the surface, with steam shooting from them ~ so hot you could cook a meal over them. Great deposits of bright yellow sulfur were gathered in large areas indicating the hellish intense heat which lay beneath. The volcano has been active, this time, since January 1983.

Hawaiians believe Pele, the Goddess of Fire, created the islands. Their superstitions are many. They believe their ancestors are reincarnated as sharks. Still, they have an admirable attitude toward nature, much like the American Native Indians. Even their children have a certain wisdom and respect for their natural environment.

I was surfing on a beach in Makaha and had taken a spill on some rocks. Blood was trickling down my leg. I didn't think anything of it. It was a common occurrence with novice surfers, of which I qualified. A small Hawaiian boy, maybe six years old, walked up and solemnly pointed to my bloody leg and said, "No go back in water!" I asked why. He pointed out beyond the reef stating, "shark come!" I decided to take my small brown guardian angel's advice and bathe in the sunshine for a while.

A Rain Forest

On the Big Island we had to spend several nights in a rain forest, which is like living in a perpetually foggy and drizzly world. It was difficult to keep our bedding and equipment dry. The night temperatures would drop and we would wake up with a good dusting of snow on us.

Within minutes of the sun coming up, the snow would melt and we were right back like the day before: foggy and drizzly.

A Drowning

Two buddies from Kalamazoo, Michigan, Tim Skinner and Larry Johnson, and I were snorkeling in a beautiful lagoon on the Big Island. We had made several dives, each time chipping off pieces of coral and bringing them to the surface. We didn't have a clue as to what we were going to do with them, but nonetheless we were having a great time at it. The water was crystal clear and the bottom, at about twelve feet, was covered with colorful coral and abundant plant life. The fish were of many different species and their colors ran the spectrum.

Several times, as I paddled along the surface looking down through my mask, I had tasted salt water from my snorkel's mouthpiece. It was leaking. I made a mental note and figured I would check it out on my next trip up. I continued on until I spotted the beautiful cluster of coral I had been looking for. I had seen it on my last dive but didn't have enough air to chip it loose and carry it up. Now I dove down, paddling hard to make it to the twelve feet or so. I took my knife from it's sheath and began hacking away at the base of the coral, which at it's widest, was probably a foot in diameter. It was then I suddenly felt like I was going to throw up.

An instant later came a dreaded feeling we've all had; when we know throwing up is a certainty. A split second later I did, in one violent motion, throw up: twelve feet underwater.

My next act was, of course, the natural thing to do. I involuntarily gulped water into my lungs: salt water. It was painful. But with the pain, there quickly came upon me, a most powerful feeling of well being. My brain had kicked in with some kind of God given mechanism to comfort me as I was drowning. With this sensation, I was devoid of any pain or fear. I recall how it felt to be conscious of my situation, yet totally unconcerned with trying to change it. There I was, suspended happily in la-la land. I could see Skinner and Johnson swimming like crazy trying to get to me and all I could think was, "man, this feels great!" They grabbed me by my arms and hauled me to the surface. As soon as they got me on the beach, Skinner brought me back into the realm of the living. In coming back, I had to deal with more pain as I choked up the saltwater. To this day I am thankful to Tim Skinner and Larry Johnson for saving my life, and I must say, from that day on my fear of drowning is non-existent. Of course, I have no desire to leave this wonderful world, but the actual fear of the act of drowning does not exist in me. It was such a glorious experience.

A Feast

My friend Woodard was hiking on the Big Island, when he came upon some mountain goats. On a whim, he took aim with his M-16 rifle and killed one of them, which he managed to carry to his jeep and bring back to our camp. One of the other guys had considerable experience at deer hunting, so he field dressed the animal. We built a large fire and a makeshift rotisserie and slow cooked the goat by turning it over the red hot coals, while coating it with a gallon of barbecue sauce.

We commandeered a hundred pound bag of potatoes from the mess hall, spreading them around throughout the coals. When it was all prepared, we had a feast. Some of the men were a little skeptical at first, having never had goat before. I had eaten it many times growing up in Valier Patch. After a couple bites, the others were sold on it. The cookout was a great success.

Death In Paradise

As much as Hawaii is an authentic paradise, it can also be a dangerous place. The Department of Tourism doesn't like for this kind of talk to get out, but many local people have long hated the white man or haole (pronounced how-o-lee).

Lets face it, these are the people who killed poor old Captain Cook in 1779. Part of me understands the local people's position. When you see or read what Hawaii was back then, compared with today: all the hotels and clip joints trying to separate the pale white tourists from there greenbacks, it parallels with the history of their mainland brothers, our own Native Americans. Nevertheless, as beautiful as it is and perfect as the climate is, Hawaii can be a hazard if one is in the wrong place at the wrong time.

As a military policeman, I saw a lot of violence on Oahu. Hotel Street in Honolulu is, or at least was when I was there in the 70s, a cesspool of whores, pimps, gypsy cheats, bars and massage parlors. Payday weekends were, of course, the worst. The place was packed with servicemen.

I've got to admit, I've never met anybody in the Air Force who wasn't decent and good. You just never had any trouble out of those fly boys. But the Army, Navy, and Marines? For the most part they were trouble looking for more trouble. Then when they got a few belts down, look out! One of the biggest problems on Hotel Street were the She/Hes. These were men dressed and made up as women. Many of them looked quite convincing. They would lure drunk servicemen into dark alleys with promises of sex and then by any means take their money, which usually consisted of the soldier's entire pay.

Dealing with the military had its difficult moments but dealing with the locals was a different matter. They didn't have to be drunk to be mean. Off duty one evening, some friends and I were having a beer at a hotel lounge over on the north shore. We were talking and having a few laughs when a local boy at the end of the bar decided he didn't like haoles (whites) and threw a glass ashtray in our direction. It missed my head by inches but, with a sickening thud, made contact against the eye of my friend Woodard.

Then all hell broke loose. I found myself on the floor beneath a guy twice my size. Luckily for me, he was drunk. Each time he swung his huge fist down in the direction of my face, it was as though in slow motion. I would parry the blow and then reach up and slam my fist onto the side of his head. The problem with this system was: my blows were doing no damage. This guy was a tank. Even though he was drunk, he was still heavy and I was tiring down fast. I glanced around to find my pals in the same situation I was in, not losing the fight, but definitely not winning either. Hotel security and police finally came and broke the whole mess up. We got Woodard to an emergency room where he took 14 stitches to his eyeball.

Being in law enforcement, we were involved with crime scenes on Schofield Barracks as well as off post. A couple, walking on the beach at the north shore one morning, discovered the body of a young man, face down in the sand. He had been shot five times in the back of his head. Investigation revealed he was a marine who had been on the island just 3 days. Because he was military, we were dispatched to the scene. His killers were easily tracked down.

An autopsy revealed: mere moments before his death, he had consumed a Big Mac with fries. The police went to the closest McDonalds and showed his I.D. picture to the employees, from the night before. One recognized him and placed him with a couple of local thugs. They had been sitting with him and, more than likely, left with him. A stakeout was set up and a couple nights later, these two killers showed up. Of course, once the police separated them, each began to blame the other. I would imagine they're both still doing time.

A Hanging

My patrol partner and I were dispatched to Kolekole Pass, where a large cross stood: *(Figure 48).*

Figure 48: The cross on Kolekole Pass. A group forced it's removal, claiming it violated separation of church and state.

When we arrived, we were overcome by the stench of death. Some hikers had discovered a poor soul hanging from a tree. He had been there for a while, as the state of decomposition was advanced. His neck was stretched to about three times its normal length and was the color of a rotten banana. His feet had swelled, causing his tennis shoes to split at the seams. We had to tape off the entire area, and wait for the Crime Scene investigators to arrive. It made for a long day.

At the base of the tree this poor fellow was hanging from, sat a glass jar with the lid tightly secured. Inside was a note, along with his military I.D. card. He had explained in detail why he was ending his life. It all had to to with lost love and loneliness.

For many years, people believed the cross on Kolekole Pass had been placed there after WWII, to commemorate a Japanese pilot who, while en route to Pearl Harbor on December 7, 1941, was shot down while attacking Schofield Barracks. This is all myth.

The Japanese attack planes didn't fly through Kolekole Pass. They flew in along the Wainanae Mountain Range. Also, the Japanese strafed only a few buildings at Schofield (some think they were merely testing their guns) as they approached their true target, Wheeler Airfield, across the highway from Schofield. The film "From Here To Eternity" perpetuates this myth, as does the film "Tora Tora Tora." The soldiers at Schofield Barracks had been conducting Easter Services there for years. A cross of some sort had been there since the 1920s. After WWII a 25 foot cross was erected; then in 1962 it was replaced with a 37 foot steel cross. The cross is clearly visible in the film, "Tora Tora Tora" as the Japanese fly over Oahu. Today the cross is gone. A group of local citizens claimed it violated the separation of church and state.

Like Robinson Crusoe

In 1976, the movie "King Kong" was released. It starred Jeff Bridges and Jessica Lange. I went to see it, and in the scene where the characters first arrive on Skull Island, I was hit with a familiarity of the locale. When Jeff Bridges and Jessica Lange ran under a natural bridge near a waterfall, my suspicions were confirmed.

Figure 49: The Na Pali Coast of Kauai, Hawaii. 4000 foot cliffs; golden sand, lush vegetation and sweet cold waterfalls.

The location was the Na Pali Coast of Kauai, Hawaii: *(Figure 49)*. The natural bridge was the Honopu Arch, leading into the Honopu Valley. Several other films have also been made in the Honopu Valley, including the "Jurassic Park" films. This place was familiar to me because I had spent a week of solitude there a few years earlier.

159

It all began when I made a routine traffic stop one night. The subject's vehicle was swerving quite a bit. The gentleman behind the wheel was a Warrant Officer: a helicopter pilot. His name was John and he was as drunk as a skunk.

Knowing how people did imbibe from time to time, I was never quick to make an arrest, unless the drunk was mean and gave me a hard time. I placed John in the back seat of the patrol car. My partner followed behind in John's car. We took him home. John's wife met us at the door. We helped him upstairs and poured him into bed.

A couple days later while on patrol I was called into the MP station. Waiting to see me was: John. He thanked me for the break I had given him, and said if there was ever anything he could do for me, I should only ask. Then he told me if I ever wanted to go up in his chopper to give him a call. It wasn't long before I took him up on the offer.

Within the week I was up there with John and his co-pilot zipping around Oahu in a Huey. You haven't seen Hawaii till you've seen it by air. On our second trip out, we ventured away from Oahu and flew around the Island of Kauai. While flying around Kauai, I spotted a beach area where the cliffs climbed up four thousand feet. It was the Na Pali Coast and was accessible only by air or boat. I made a comment to John about how "I'd love to spend a week there sometime." John replied, "We can help you make it happen."

What had started out as an offhanded wishful statement was suddenly reeling in my head. I began planning my Robinson Crusoe experience in earnest. I couldn't help but wonder if John and his buddy could get in trouble for taking part in this adventure.

In 1970, while I was stationed at Fort Knox, there had been an incident in which an Army Captain, a helicopter pilot, flew his Huey helicopter from Ft. Knox to Cleveland, Ohio where he landed on an elementary school playground (with children present) which happened to sit right next door to the home of his parents. Phone calls were made and his butt was in deep hot water. He was arrested by the local police and personnel were dispatched from Fort Knox to Cleveland to retrieve the chopper.

My little outing was going to take place on the Na Pali Coast of Kauai, with nothing or nobody in sight. I had peace of mind no one would suffer any repercussions. When I got back to Schofield Barracks, I went straight to my company's orderly room and put in a request for a one week leave.

I had John's flight schedule so it was all co-ordinated. On the assigned day I met the guys at Wheeler Airfield and we took off. I had a duffel bag with plenty of provisions, including some C rations, cigarettes, blankets, suntan lotion, and other odds and ends. About 120 miles later we came into the beach area. The guys sat down and off went my duffel bag, with me right behind it. In no time, the chopper was gone and the only sound was the surf beating against the shore. The place was paradise. I felt as though I was the only human on earth.

The first thing I did was build a small hut. I covered it with the large elephant ear leaves which were plentiful. I had been a Boy Scout, so I knew a lot of survival technics, however when it came to securing fire, I wasn't taking any chances. Just to be on the safe side, I had taken along several cigarette lighters and matches. I gathered firewood and built a small fire. By the time the sun went down, my little campsite already had a lived in look. I had all I needed for my short stay.

As my first day had been spent making a home in my new paradise, I was beat. Too tired to eat. The first night I slept like I had never slept before. There is definitely something therapeutic about the sound of an ocean surf pounding repeatedly on a sandy shore. I awoke the first morning while the sun was barely up, and I was famished. I enjoyed a C Ration meal of ham and beans with crackers and a chocolate bar. I drank the sweet cold water from the waterfall. Just to wake myself up good and proper, I went down to the beach and jumped into the cold crystal blue water. It was just what I needed to start my day. I made it a tradition each morning.

Being alone in an uninhabited area can really bring you in touch with the Creator. This place made me so much more aware of His Works.

The first full day, I caught some fish with a net. I seasoned these with salt and pepper and wrapped them in broad leaves. Then I packed the whole thing with mud. Placed in the red hot coals of my fire, they slow cooked all day to perfection. It was delicious. Right out of my Boy Scout Manual. I had fish every day. I explored the thick jungle like overgrowth at the base of the mountains, and I swam a lot. I had to be cautious while swimming. The undertows were strong, and if I wasn't careful I could be pulled out to sea.

The days went by slowly, as I had hoped they would. During my stay I never once saw a boat and only a couple planes, thousands of feet in the air. One day it rained. I sat in my dry, little hut and watched it for a long time. Then, as is the case in Hawaii, the sun came out with the most beautiful rainbow. A spectrum of colors more vivid than I had ever seen. During my stay I was reminded of Henry David Thoreau's "Walden." I had read it years earlier with the encouragement of my neighbor Miss Grace Seiler,

"I went to the woods because I wished to live deliberately, to front only the essential facts of life, and see if I could not learn what it had to teach, and not, when I came to die, discover that I had not lived."
From "Walden" or "Life In The Woods"
by David Henry Thoreau

The reading had gone far over my head as a young boy, but here in this place thoreau's meaning became clear. I ventured up as high as I could into the vegetation on the mountain sides. Various fruits grew wild there. I saw several goats scaling the steep sides of the mountains, as though their hooves were suction cups. Thick fluffy white clouds would linger on the sides of the cliffs, the mountains holding them at bay. Strong winds would then come along and carry the clouds up and away, and on and on it went.

During my island getaway, one day felt like three. I was calm and rested. I sat on the beach, contemplating the immensity of God's creation. The ocean, the mountains, and a sky reaching out toward an endless horizon. Then there was me.

A part of me wanted to stay there forever. I think there is in each person a desire to exist in a place like the Na Pali Coast. John had given me an estimated time for their arrival. Still, all kinds of random thoughts were running through my mind. I knew they wouldn't forget me, but what if they were grounded for some reason. What if the Huey helicopter was out of commission. What if...?

Practicality didn't make it's way into those first flights of fancy, but then reality hit me with a little speck in the sky. Soon came the sound of rotor blades. In no time the Huey sat down long enough for me to hop on and we lifted off. Sitting in the chopper's open bay door with my legs dangling out at 2000 feet, I was on my way back to Schofield Barracks a different person. I had spent seven days with no distractions between me and my Creator. After Johnston Atoll and my time on Kauai, Schofield Barracks: *(Figures 50 & 51)* seemed like a living hell.

Figure 50: One of the several quads at Schofield Barracks, Hawaii.

Figure 51: An aerial shot of the quads at Schofield Barracks.

165

Chapter 9

My Motorcycle

Shortly after I settled in with my new unit in Hawaii, I bought a motorcycle. A beautiful 450 Honda, robin's egg blue with white trim. My pals, Skinner and Johnson had their own bikes, so along with a few others we would make the rounds of Oahu. We would cruise the North Shore and sometimes stop along the way to watch the hippies who would congregate on a cliff there. The hippies would be smoking pot and taking turns jumping into a natural pool that separated the highway from the cliff. Occasionally, a bus full of tourists would stop, and the visitors would be treated to a real show.

When they had a sizable audience, the hippies would do all sorts of acrobatics and more than usual dangerous stunts. Watching the hippies going through their motions and the tourists standing there with us, their cameras clicking away at the surreal scene, I couldn't help but think how the hippies were a lot like monkeys in a zoo.

We would finally make our way to Waikiki, where there was so much going on, a person felt cheated if he couldn't take it all in at once. The International Market Place was the center of the action. There were restaurants and shops galore.

We would sit for a long while and watch the Hare Krishnas as they danced up and down the sidewalk. There would be 30 or more, with shaved heads, colorful robes, no shoes, all carrying a tambourine and chanting some tune which, regardless of its message, was really quite catchy. I had to give those people credit for consistency. They were out there every night, rain or clear skies. I'm not sure if they were recruiting or not, but it did seem to me their numbers increased considerably over time.

Wam Bam

One afternoon I was riding my 450. Just moments earlier I had picked it up from a motorcycle shop. I had gotten new tires, a tune up, and a few other odds and ends fixed on the bike. As I approached an intersection on Schofield Barracks, I saw a car sitting at a stop sign. Little did I know, the car's driver did not see me. At the exact same second I arrived at the intersection, the driver bolted out and BAM!!

I don't remember the impact ~ being torn away over the handlebars ~ flying across the car hood or hitting the pavement. I do recall suddenly lying on my back with a horde of people standing over me, one of them asking, "Is he dead?" I heard a woman screaming in broken English: "He was speeding, he was speeding!" Then I heard someone else say, "No, he wasn't!!" Then the woman started yelling, "I didn't see him! I didn't see him!" This all served as good testimony during the insurance depositions.

There was no pain at first. Then two overly helpful bystanders tried to remove my Bell helmet. Suddenly, my entire body reacted painfully. An ambulance arrived, and I was scraped off the pavement and taken to the dispensary. There, I was examined by a doctor who did nothing more than lift and push and pull, making notes of what made me   cry out in agony. A nurse cut my clothing away and then covered me with a sheet, from my neck down. I was placed on a gurney and rolled out to the heliport and then moved, yet again, to a stretcher and placed on the chopper with the main rotor blade creating a small wind storm.

Once on board, we took off for Tripler Army Medical Center. With both bay doors open, at an altitude of 2000 feet, the sheet covering me was flapping in the wind. All I could manage to mutter to the medic sitting beside me was, "Please don't let me fall out." He promised me he wouldn't. I was not comforted by his words.

Tripler Army Medical is a massive place. Bright coral pink in color, it sits high atop a mountain, in full view of Honolulu. I would spend a long time there as my injuries healed. Once we arrived at TAMC, I was painfully x-rayed. I was then taken to the department where plaster casts were applied. It took quite awhile, as several casts had to be created, covering almost my entire left side. I was taken into surgery where the doctor's pieced my left heel back together: more pain. By the time I was rolled into a hospital ward, with a dozen or so other men and put to bed, I was worn out. I was then hooked up to an I.V., and an apparatus dispensing pain killer. Soon I was out like a light.

All in all, my entire left side had taken the brunt of the damage. I had a broken left clavicle; four broken ribs, left arm broken in two places, left leg broken in three places, a dislocated hip, and a shattered left heel. The entire left side of my body was one big purple bruise and not to let my right side feel left out: I was hurting all over.

My first morning there I was drugged up pretty good, looking like some kind of creature, half man/half plaster. A nurse walked up to the foot of my bed and glanced at my chart. She then looked at me and asked, "Who are you?" I replied, "Gary Owens." She stared at me suspiciously and told me in no uncertain terms: *you are **not** Gary Owens."* I was doped up considerably, and I had been through an awful lot in the past several hours, but still I was positive I was who I thought I was. One thing was for sure. I was perplexed. The nurse then called over a couple other nurses and demanded to know what was going on. They began their little investigation, and in a matter of minutes the mystery was solved. It seems my hospital bed had been previously occupied by one Gary Owens, Specialist Fourth Class, 25th Infantry Division, victim of a motorcycle accident: identical to my case. He had been there for nearly two months and had been discharged mere hours before I was admitted. Needless to say, we were all amazed at those incredible circumstances. It was the talk of the hospital for several days.

The healing process was slow. After a couple months the casts started coming off. Old casts off, new casts on. Then came the physical therapy. As soon as I was able to make a half decent effort at rolling out of bed, I was taken daily to a large clinic where there were dozens of people in varying degrees of recuperating from some kind of injury. It was painful, using parts of my body, broken then mended, now being made to function as though no injury ever occurred. Rehab was slow. My stay there was not restful.

Once a week they'd show a movie in our ward. Just off the bay, there was a lanai facing the mountains. It was a great place to just sit and ponder one's life. Tripler was nice, but I wanted to get back to my unit. After some time, the doctors relented and agreed: I could go back to Schofield Barracks on limited duty status only.

A Close Call

I was still wearing what was called a figure eight brace around my shoulders, as my left clavicle had not completely mended. I couldn't go on regular patrol duty, so I was placed in charge of the arms room. I spent each night there from six P.M. to six A.M. My job was handing out and taking in the .45 caliber pistols used on MP duty. The job was boring. The only notable incident almost cost me my life.

Before an MP could turn in his pistol, he was required to clear it, that is: remove the magazine of rounds; point the weapon into a barrel filled with sand and pull the trigger, then lock the slide back before turning it in to me. One morning a joker came in having failed to follow those simple steps. Just as he started to hand me his weapon, a round was discharged missing my head by a couple inches. The bullet went into the concrete wall behind my head and the guy who had fired it stood there in shock. A couple other guys who were present, were frozen in disbelief. I reached across the desk and carefully removed the pistol from his hand, because a second round had gone into the chamber after the first round was ejected.

After emptying the weapon and clearing it, I grabbed the shooter by his shirt and went ballistic with, "You stupid bastard, you almost killed me." The guy was in shock from the round going off.

171

A .45 pistol is loud anywhere, but in a small indoor area, it leaves your ears ringing. I realized this was a serious matter. The Army deals severely, with personnel who illegally discharge a firearm. On one hand, I wanted to punch this guy out and leave him hanging in the wind, but I didn't. I closed the doors to the arms room and told the three of them I would not report it to the authorities. If I did, the careless shooter, their friend, would likely be punished with an Article 15, causing him to lose a fair amount of freedom and money. I swore them all to secrecy and told them they could never mention the incident to anyone, ever, even in a casual conversation. Mr. Shooter promised he would never do something so stupid again. He apologized repeatedly to me.

I took a sheet of paper, some directive from Division or whatever and taped it over the bullet hole. From that day on, I insisted pistols be taken apart and cleaned before approaching my desk. The men raised a stink about it, but it finally became second nature for them.

I think the reason I went out of my way for that kid was simple enough. If I had been in his boots, the one thing I would have wanted more than anything would have been mercy!

Soon, I was allowed to go back on patrol duty. As luck would have it, my first patrol partner was the shooter. We got along just fine, and neither one of us ever brought up the shooting incident.

Music In Hawaii

While at Schofield Barracks, I was still working on my songwriting skills. Some evenings I would sit out on the lanai and play my guitar and sing. My buddies would gather around and listen, and they were complimentary of my singing. There were a couple other guys in my company who played and sang. We would have little jam sessions and really get into it. They were big fans of Hank Williams Sr., and some other country artists, so we had a real common thread.

One day, some friends told me about some auditions Special Services were having at the Schofield Barracks service club. It seemed the Army was putting together a country band to travel around, playing all the service clubs in the Pacific Islands. Friends encouraged me to make the audition, but I didn't go out of pure insecurity.

A band, called "Rambling Country" was finally formed. I didn't find out until years later, the fellow chosen as the lead singer was non other than country music superstar George Strait: *(Figure 52)*. He was stationed at Schofield Barracks the exact same years I was there.

*Figure 52: Country music superstar George Strait.
Stationed at Schofield Barracks, Hawaii the same years I
was there. We never know who we walk among, do we?*

A Talent Dies

Mackey Feary: *(Figure 53)* was an up and coming singer/songwriter when we met in 1973. I had stopped by a Honolulu recording studio one day to talk about booking a session.

Figure 53: Mackey Feary. Singer/song writer. Gone too soon.

At the time, Mackey was a member of a band called Kalapana. Some of the local singers were making great headway in their careers. A duo known as Cecilio & Kapono had gotten a major label deal and were riding high with a hit song. Kalapana opened for C & K when they appeared at the bandshell in the park. The local clubs were showcasing the talents of all these young guys. Mackey Feary was as kind and helpful as a person could be. I was

175

happy for him when I saw later he was experiencing some success. We would run into one another from time to time and Mackey always had a great attitude about music and life.

Sadly, Mackey Feary became hooked on methamphetamines and after being given several chances by the courts to beat the habit, he was arrested after threatening his wife with a hammer in an effort to get money for drugs. Mackey was sentenced to ten years in prison.

At one of his shows, a few weeks prior, he had stood on stage and proclaimed his addiction and swore to overcome it. He said he was recovering. Someone who had known Mackey for many years was overheard to say, "He'll never make it. He's got too many friends."

Mackey Feary hanged himself in his prison cell in February 1999.

Chapter 10

Meat & Three

I got out of the Army the second time in May of 1975. I had received a little money from an insurance settlement on my motorcycle accident, and I knew just what I wanted to do with it ~ open a restaurant. It was really a repeat of my country music promotion dream. You buy food, cook it, serve it to customers, and make money. I rented a small place in the south end of Mount Vernon, Illinois. I called it "Ye Old Lantern."

It was a meat and three. When I was working on the place, getting it ready to open, my greatest fear was, I would open and no one would come! Just the opposite happened. I opened in October of 1975 to a packed breakfast, and then when lunch came around it started all over again. The breakfast and lunch crowds just kept on growing. I was taking in a lot of money, but it seemed by the time all expenses were paid, including payroll and rent, I wasn't making anything at all. I was getting up at four in the morning and opening at six. I was working myself to death and wasn't making a decent salary for myself. I finally had to make the decision to close down.

In retrospect, I saw where I had gone wrong. Lack of business know-how is the prime reason most small businesses fail: especially restaurants. Of the top five businesses most likely to fail the first year, a restaurant is number one. I have since, over the years, spoken with several small restaurant owners and they all agree: as the owner, you have to sit at the cash register with a good view of the back door. That's a big part of the success of a restaurant.

Viva Las Vegas

After shutting down the restaurant, I decided to head out to Las Vegas, Nevada, to become a slot machine mechanic. Probably about now you're thinking, this guy sure was scattered! Well I'm the first to agree. I had known a fella in the army who had been a slot machine mechanic at one of the big casinos, and he had all kinds of great things to say about the money, and working conditions. So, on a whim, once again, I was on my way.

My old 1964 Chevy didn't have a radio, so I did a lot of singing to myself from Mount Vernon, Illinois, to Denver, Colorado. I was determined to save as much money as possible driving out, so I'd have a little something to live on. Driving across Kansas I began to hallucinate. Lying before me were hundreds of thousands of acres of bare ground, where the occasional small speck of a white house would appear in the distance. I would see the image of a man standing up ahead, on the shoulder of the highway; then as I got closer it would magically transform into a mailbox. This went on for quite a while. Finally I came to a small town sitting in the middle of nowhere called Burlington. As I was getting gas I asked how much further it was to Colorado. I discovered I was 12 miles into Colorado. I suppose I had expected to cross the state line and suddenly have the Rocky Mountains appear. I was still a long way from Denver, and when I finally did arrive, it was snowing. I was advised not to attempt crossing the Rockies that night. I spent the night drinking coffee in a truck stop and caught a few winks in my car. By the following morning, the roads had been cleared. I continued on.

After driving a while, I noticed my little six cylinder Chevy was having a hard time getting up some of the steeper grades. I stopped at a garage, and a fella told me I was running too rich in fuel because of the thinner air. He adjusted my carburetor, and he didn't charge me a dime. In no time I was back on the road.

Coming out of the Eisenhower Tunnel, I came upon a fella thumbing a ride. He had a backpack and sleeping bag, and one of his legs was bandaged up with a bloody shirt. I picked him up. I don't pick up hitchhikers these days, but this was over 30 years ago ~ a much different world. The guy was from Queens, New York. He was making his way to Los Angeles. I asked him what happened to his leg.

He explained how the night before, he had been standing on the side of the road, in the blinding snowstorm, with his thumb out. He saw two headlights coming toward him; when they got to him he was suddenly picked up off the ground and thrown through the air ~ over the guardrail, into a rocky ravine. Too late, he had found out, it was a snow plow with the blade extending out about four feet on each side. He managed to climb back up to get his things, and then made his way to an old abandoned copper mining tool shed where he wrapped his leg and spent the night.

The next morning, he climbed back up to the road, where I came along. Being without a radio, I welcomed someone to talk to and talk he did. I thought he would never shut up. He told me all about his venture thus far. I asked him why he didn't just take a Greyhound or fly to L.A! There was "no adventure in that," he said. I had to agree.

After hours of driving, I was hungry, and I figured this guy was too. I had $500 on me, but I didn't want him to know that. I figured he had some money as well and was probably feeling as cautious toward me. Somewhere, among the huge stone mountains of Utah, we saw a sign advertising ten hamburgers for a dollar. That was just what I was looking for. We stopped and picked up ten hamburgers and a couple cokes. We each acted like it was the last of our money as we paid up. Soon, we were back on the road.

The desert can play tricks on you at night. I was driving along, and as I came over a ridge I saw lights. Like a million lights; the colors of rubies, emeralds, and white diamonds. My passenger said, "There's Vegas." I said something about how glad I was that we had finally made it. I then saw a sign that read Las Vegas 46 miles. It looked close enough to reach out and touch.

As soon as we reached the strip in Vegas, my passenger got out and thanked me for the ride. I had just hauled the guy over 800 miles, and I was thankful that he had kept me from going stir crazy on the last leg of my journey. He had served his purpose. I was in Las Vegas. At last!

I got a room, and early the next day I went to check out the Slot Machine Mechanic School. It was VA approved, 18 months long with a guaranteed job placement. I wanted to make sure I had a job while going to school so I went to the first big hotel I came to ~ The MGM Grand.

This was the hotel Lowe's Inc. opened after getting out of the major movie making business. They had sold off all their assets: property, costumes, and props, including Dorothy's Ruby slippers from "The Wonderful Wizard of Oz." So here I was applying for a job in security and the same day they scheduled me for a physical and uniform fitting. I passed the physical with flying colors. When I went for the uniform fitting, I discovered I would be dressed like some kind of town marshal, complete with western hat, boots, and vest with badge, and a six shooter with holster tied down at the hip. I was even expected to wear a bandanna tied just so-so around my neck. I was scheduled for a training session in a couple days, so I took the free time to see some of the sights.

Las Vegas was a strange town. The job turnover is great because many people can't resist the gambling. They get upside down in debt. In the newspaper, there were literally hundreds of notices of Gamblers Anonymous groups meeting. The newspapers were full of real estate listings like 3 BR, 2BA Stucco w/pool. Nothing Down with E-Z monthly payments. I hit a couple casinos, the Golden Nugget being the largest at the time.

I watched a mixture of free wheeling tourists playing slots, who perhaps came with a certain amount of money they could lose, along side some poor overworked looking little waitress, who had just gotten off work and was trying desperately to turn her tips into a small fortune. With a cigarette dangling from her lips, the lady had six machines tied up and was feverishly going from one to another. I didn't like what I saw in Vegas. When the sun went down, Vegas lit up like a carnival. The cold air rushed out from the large casinos to cool the pedestrians along the sidewalks. Neon wrapped many of the casinos; literally millions of light bulbs lined the strip. I had once read in a book on advertising: anything that moves, lights up or makes noise could be sold: Las Vegas in spades. During the day, the ugly brown desert and scrub grass were glaring with the tired sleepless people making their way from one joint to the next. Even during daylight hours the lights are on. They never turn them off.

The casinos had eating establishments in them where you could get a full breakfast for fifty nine cents or a steak and baked potato for ninety nine cents. The concept? Keep them in the casino.

It was all too E-Z. I didn't care for Vegas. I called the MGM folks and said thanks but no thanks. I didn't want to play cowboy. I packed my few belongings into my overworked Chevy, and headed on back to Illinois. A few minutes outside Vegas, on the southern route, I stopped and stood looking out off Hoover Dam. I had a bunch of road maps in my car, and about then I was really wishing I had a map to get me through life.

The trip back to Illinois seemed to take forever. I was going back after yet another failed venture. I knew I couldn't make it in southern Illinois, but then, I wasn't making it *anywhere.*

Once back home, I worked in a factory to stay alive, planning my next move. I was going to tackle what I had feared for a long time. I believe my poor track record, failure upon failure, finally put me in a state of mind where I was saying to myself, "If I have to be a failure, I want to be doing what I really feel in my soul I was meant to do. I was going to Nashville, Tennessee ~ to write songs.

Chapter 11

Nashville I

When I arrived in Nashville in May of 1976, it was raining hard at about one o'clock in the morning. I was in my trusty '64 Chevy, and I had with me my Epiphone guitar, a few clothes, and a couple hundred bucks.

I stumbled upon a greasy spoon behind the main post office on Broadway. It was aptly named the U.S. Meal. It smelled like a mix of cigarette smoke, grease, and burnt coffee. The place was empty except for a tired looking waitress and a rather old busboy/cook. While scarfing down a hamburger, I asked the waitress several questions related to my coming to town. Where's Music Row? The Grand Ole Opry? Where do they tape Hee Haw? Do country singin' stars ever come in here? She responded to each of my inquiries with indifference. It made me wonder if Music City was all I had made it out to be. Neither of them had ever been to Opryland. The old cook asked me, "Ain't that the place thats got that loopty loop?" I didn't know.

I spent my first night in my car, in a parking lot off Eighth Avenue. With the rain pounding down on the roof, I slept like a rock. I awoke the next morning to the sounds of men slamming their car

184

doors and talking. I had parked adjacent to a machine shop, and it was time for work. My first business of the day was to find a room. I got a newspaper and called several "room for rent" numbers. Most were just too expensive. Finally, I called one in which an elderly lady asked me if I was a drinking man. I assured her I was not, to any great degree. Then she told me the rent was a hundred dollars per month: I could pay by the week. She gave me directions.

The house: *(Figure 54)* was a large stately place with twelve foot ceilings. It had seen better days. My landlady's name was Mrs. Hulick. She was eighty years old and had the kindest, sweetest spirit.

Figure 54: "Lookaway." The former home of Beth Slater Whitson. This is where I lived when I first arrived in Nashville in 1976.

The house had belonged to Mrs. Hulick's aunt, Beth Slater Whitson: *(Figure 55)* the writer of an American classic song, entitled "Let Me Call You Sweetheart."

Figure 55: Beth Slater Whitson (R) and her sister Alice (L) with their family. Beth wrote "Let Me Call You Sweetheart."

She had written many others, but that one became a legendary standard. Beth Slater Whitson and her sister Alice, who was a writer in her own right, moved to Nashville in 1913. When Beth married in 1916 her husband gave her the home as a wedding present. She named the place "Lookaway." In 1930, she passed away in the home. Her funeral was conducted there. By the time I came onto the scene, the house sat in the middle of a poor run down section of east Nashville.

186

Mrs. Hulick recalled visiting her Aunts Beth and Alice, when she was but 17 years old. "Back then," she said, "from the front porch of Lookaway, downtown Nashville sat far off in the distance, with nothing lying in between but trees and the Cumberland River."

I got a job within the week working security at the Country Music Foundation. The job gave me a chance to educate myself in and around all aspects of the music business, past, present, and future. I was fortunate that my boss, Barbara Saunders and her husband, Greg, were kind enough to invite me to their home in Lakewood for dinner one evening. It was there I met Barb's brother, Arliss Scott: *(Figure 56)*.

Figure 56: My friend Arliss Scott.

Home spun philosopher and guitar picker.

Arliss passed away on Nov. 15, 2004.

Arliss was a left-handed guitar picker who played a right handed guitar, with the guitar upside down. He had worked for several years on the road, with all the big stars. He was an accomplished studio musician as well. Arliss Scott played a bigger part in helping me to learn the craft of songwriting than any other person.

Arliss hailed from Youngstown, Ohio. He had come to Nashville at a fairly young age, and with his talent he found work immediately as a guitar player. He was a philosopher of sorts; could discuss any topic with anyone. He once told me he hadn't planned to be a musician at all. When he was a kid, he had dreamed of being an archaeologist. Had he gone that way in life, I'm sure he would have made a fine one.

By the time I met Arliss he had already gotten his fill of the music business, with its glad handing and insincere B.S. I used his cautionary tales as a guide, to protect myself from the things he hated about Nashville's famous (or infamous) Music Row.

I stayed with Mrs. Hulick for about two months. The rent was more than reasonable, and Mrs. Hulick was a wonderful kind lady, but there were four other boarders staying there as well, and they were less than wonderful. One fella was going through a divorce. He was angry about everything. Another was an out of work house siding salesman, always bugging me for a ride somewhere. I did what had become so easy for me. I moved.

My next landlady was named Pauline. Eighty-six going on thirty-nine. She lived in the fashionable Continental Apartments on West End Avenue. The room she had for rent was quite a steal at one hundred and fifty dollars per month.

Pauline had been voted Miss Detroit in 1926, and on the white baby grand piano in her living room lay various newspaper clippings and photos of her from that period. When I made note of them, she feigned embarrassment, saying she had gotten them out earlier in the day, to show someone and just hadn't had the time to put them away. They lay there on the white baby grand for the next three months. I would hear Pauline explain their presence to visitors who came around from time to time.

One of those visitors was someone who became a great friend to me ~ Fay Dickinson: *(Figure 57)*. Fay was one of the most giving, sincere human beings I've ever known. If a friend were down and out in the middle of nowhere, they could count on Fay to show up with an army of people to help. She was a collector of people. She knew the rich and dignified, as well as the poor, still holding on to their dignity.

Fay considered it rude to ask a person what they did for a living. It gave the impression their answer would be factored into what one thought of them. To Fay, all honest work, was honorable work.

Figure 57: My dear friend Fay Dickinson. I describe her purpose in life in one word : Others.

She would throw dinner parties and invite some of her friends. I found myself, on many occasions, sitting at a table with ten or so others from all walks of life. A University professor would be seated next to a gasoline station attendant. A botanist would be sitting across from a manicurist. The conversations rolled.

The only prerequisite for Fay to take a liking to you: *you had to be real.* No phonies were allowed. Over the years I saw Fay help many people with no regard for what it cost her in time or money. Many times I was the recipient of her kindness.

190

One day I woke up feeling ill. I had moved, yet again, to a dark and dank basement apartment of an old stone house on Belmont Boulevard. I was feverish and nauseous. I lay in bed all that day in a delirium. I was so weak I could barely crawl to the bathroom. After a fitful day and night, out of desperation, I called my friend Fay. She came over immediately. She didn't leave my side for two whole days, as she tried to keep my fever down.

I don't know when she rested. I was miserable the entire time, going in and out of nightmarish fitful sleeps. Barb and Greg Saunders came by one evening. They were shocked at my condition ~ the sweating and delirious ramblings. I was so out of it. I refused to go to the hospital. Fay hung in there with me until the fever finally broke. I began to regain my strength. Fay Dickinson was that kind of friend.

Through Fay, I came to know the Bowie Sisters. Dr. Anna, Dr. Evangeline (Van), and Dr. Byrd Bowie were ages 86, 79 and 81, respectively. The Bowie sisters lived near me, one street over and a half block down, on Oakland Avenue. They had long before quit practicing medicine and were living out their lives in relative seclusion.

At first meeting them I was treated kindly, however, I was not invited into their home, so there we sat visiting one late August evening on their front porch. I was sitting in an old ladder back chair, and at one point Anna motioned for me to move to the left just a few inches. I complied but was a little baffled at the request. Van informed me how the street light had been shining in Anna's eyes; by scooting my seat over, I was shielding her from it.

Soon after meeting the sisters there was a knock on my door. It was Van: *(Figure 58)*. She wanted me to help her empty their house of a few items.

Figure 58`: My friend Dr. Evangeline "Van" Bowie. Graduation from Hume ~ Fogg High School. Nashville, Tennessee. 1919.

It was my first time to be invited inside their house. The place was filled with newspapers ~ Wall Street Journals ~ thousands of them. Medical Journals and magazines of all sorts. The entire downstairs was literally filled with stack after stack of trash. We began carrying out the newspapers but after several trips Van misjudged one of the front steps and took a bad fall. She landed in Vanderbilt Hospital with a cast on her leg. My car had recently bit the dust, so I walked from my apartment to

Vanderbilt Hospital to visit Van one evening. In her room there was a large basket of fruit. She told me she only wanted the bananas, and I should take the rest. I carried the basket home.

Two evenings later, I went back for another visit. There on the nightstand were those bananas, almost black ~ what I would call rotten. I asked her if she had lost her fondness for bananas. She informed me she was waiting for them to ripen a little more.

A few months later, after Van had regained the use of her leg, she asked if I would drive her and Anna to see some property they owned. I had just purchased another car, so off we went.

Near Fairview, Tennessee, Van told me to turn off the main highway. Suddenly we were riding on a small path like road surrounded by pine trees and three small spring fed lakes. Van explained how she had bought this land sometime in the 1950s and had since planted, by hand, over 500,000 pine trees, which she bought from the U.S. Government at the cost of ten for a penny. Van designed the road and each of the lakes. She would walk over the grounds carrying a stick, followed by a hired bulldozer. Indicating to the dozer operator where she wanted some soil removed and what areas she wanted built up. One woman with a vision and a hired bulldozer had turned an 800 acre piece of worthless land into a beautiful refuge of nature. A few days later we went to see another piece of property the sisters owned. It was wooded, and at one point we arrived at a place Van referred to as "Bowie Holler." I asked, offhandedly, if it had been been named after her family. "Well," she replied, "the Bowie part was."

Before her death in 1992 Van gave the property to the City of Fairview. Today it is the Bowie Nature Park. Seventeen miles of hiking trails and playgrounds. Of those three woman made lakes, one of them is named "Lake Van ": *(Figure 59)*.

Figure 59: My children, Justin (10) and Christen (13), catching the big ones on Lake Van. Bowie Nature Park, Fairview, Tennessee. 2008.

I made one trip with the sisters to visit their brother, Walter. He had been hospitalized for some time. He was in his seventies and quite senile. His sisters stimulated his mind by encouraging him to explain the workings of a laser. He could explain each minute detail of the workings of lasers. He could not, however, hold a conversation with anyone about anything else.

One by one, the Bowie sisters passed away. I was a better person for having known them.

Kathy Gregory

In 1977, while working security at the Country Music Foundation, I came in contact with a lady named Kathy Gregory. Kathy's claim to fame was being the widow of cowboy musician Bobby Gregory. Bobby had died about six years earlier. He had seen some success in music and film. He played the accordion and had written several songs, one of which was entitled ~ "Mama Get The Hammer, There's A Fly On Baby's Head." He also claimed to have written the classic, "Will The Circle Be Unbroken." The claim has never been substantiated.

One day, the head of public relations called upstairs and told me Kathy Gregory was on her way to the Foundation, intent on making a scene. It seems Kathy had donated several of Bobby's items to the museum, which the curator promptly stashed away in the archives room. Kathy had been insulted and her late husband defamed. Knowing Kathy lived only three blocks away, I took my position at the front entrance. Sure enough, a big older model Caddy with rusted out rocker panels pulled up front. It was Kathy Gregory. She was a tall, big boned woman, maybe 65 years old, with bright yellow hair. On this day she was decked out in all bright yellow. Pants, shirt, western hat and boots. When she got to the door, I stepped out and requested she leave. She stood her ground. I turned to walk back inside but she was right on my heels. I had to stop in the doorway to block her. I was trying to handle the situation without physical contact, but Kathy was making it nearly impossible. I finally grabbed her by her shirt sleeve and pulled her outside. I explained to her how this could only end one way, with her being arrested by Metro Police and charged with trespassing, making threats and being an all around pain in the ass. She said she was going to sue the Foundation and she was going to sue me, too. I told her to go ahead and sue me, I had nothing to lose. I guess I called her bluff. She steamed off back to her car and sped away. The next time I saw Kathy Gregory was about a year later. She was in her big ugly Cadillac, only she was riding shotgun. Behind the wheel, sat a young man decked out in the most gaudy western attire. I recall thinking, "Well, Kathy went and got herself another cowboy."

The Thompson Brothers

The Thompson Brothers, Harry and Larry, hailed from Walla Walla, Washington. For a period of several years, during the 1970s, these two characters could be seen daily as they walked along 16th Avenue's "Music Row."

They were easy to spot because they wore, year round, even on the hottest days, red and white striped pants and shirts, heavy knee length, black fur coats with tall black fur hats to match. Both were toothless. Actually, Harry did have teeth on my first meeting them. Then one day I went out to talk with them and lo and behold, Harry was toothless. They explained how Harry had gotten all his teeth pulled, so they would look identical.

One carried a guitar, the other a banjo. They were the worst awful musicians and singers one could imagine. They carried with them, 8X10 black and white glossy photos, which they were more than happy to autograph.

Their big break came one day when the producers of TVs "Hee Haw" had them on the show. It was a spoof of another popular TV show, "The Gong Show." Jr. Samples stood in front of a curtain and introduced the next act. The curtain opened to reveal "The Thompson Brothers." With their guitar and banjo at the ready, their mouths open to sing, the curtain closes as quickly as it had opened. It wasn't fifteen minutes, but it *was* fame.

Red River Dave

David McEnery: *(Figure 60)* AKA "Red River Dave" had been around a long while by the time I met him on Nashville's Music Row. Dave's greatest claim to fame was having been the first paid music star to sing on television. The year was 1939, at the New York World's Fair. Television was in it's infancy and a young handsome Red River Dave was on board.

Figure 60: Red River Dave McEnery. In his heyday. The first television star.

He had maintained a career for several years, but by the time I met Dave and his wife, he was performing as an evangelist under a small tent, using hay bales as pews. He handed out fliers which featured a picture of him throwing a lasso, with the caption: *"Red River Dave ~ Ropin' 'em in for Jesus."* He and his wife wore full western garb, along with cowboy boots, spray painted gold. They had pitched their revival tent in an empty lot on Music Row, across from the wax museum, and for several days they were a common sight cruising around in their Cadillac, as they prepared for the big event. It seems like back in the 1960s and 70s everyone in the music business drove a Cadillac. It didn't have to be a newer model, which it seldom was, as long as it was a Caddy, preferably a DeVille.

As in the case of Red River Dave's Caddy, it was covered with stickers and posters advertising his past and present. I came to meet Dave and his lovely wife when, one day, they came by the Country Music Foundation. They were sincere, I think, in their mission to spread the gospel.

I attended the first night of the tent meeting. Stepping under the small tent, I made myself comfortable on a bale of hay. As the service progressed it was obvious the two or three others there, along with me, made up the congregation. Curious tourists, making their way from one tacky amusement to another, would watch from the sidewalk for a while, then proceed on as Red River Dave and his wife gave it all they had at "ropin' 'em in for Jesus." The revival lasted only a week. I drove by one day and the tent was gone, as were the bales of hay.

Red River Dave McEnery passed away on January the 15th, 2002 at the age of 87.

Grace on New Years Eve

I have had several brushes with death in my life. Some closer than others.

On New Years Eve in 1977 I was still living in the basement apartment on Belmont Boulevard. It was snowing quite heavily. The streets were slick.

Just a few minutes before midnight, I walked down Belmont Boulevard to a phone booth at the corner of Belmont and Blair. I called my family and wished them a Happy New Year. We spoke for only a moment.

I hung up the phone, and just as I stepped from the booth, a car came sliding around the corner; bounced over the curb, crashing into the phone booth, completely destroying it. If I had stayed in the phone booth two seconds more, I would have been killed.

Chapter 12

The Music Biz

I had been knocking around Nashville for three years, working dead end jobs, which allowed me the freedom to hang out down on Music Row. My old guitar pickin' friend, Arliss Scott, had given me some good advice during my first few weeks in town. He said, "Put yourself on a five year plan; if you haven't accomplished anything noteworthy in that time, get out."

With Arliss' help, I learned the craft of songwriting. Arliss once jokingly told me, "Hey, anybody can write a great song. Just pick a great song; write new words for it and then change the melody."

He had an excellent ear for the song idea. It either worked or it didn't. If the initial idea is not great, and if there's not a great "hook," then forget it. As a studio musician, Arliss had sit in on lots of recording sessions. Many were with legitimate artists. Others, however, were no talent wannabes using superb musicians to play great "licks" on terribly composed melodies, with the worst awful lyrics.

Each time I wrote a new song, I would go play it for Arliss. He was brutally honest and it made me work harder at writing. The Nashville

Songwriter's Association used to hand out a small guide to newly arriving songwriters. Within it, were fifteen suggestions to aid writers in their quest for success. The number one rule still stands out in my mind. I myself have passed it on to many young up and comers. It basically states: "Never take the opinions of your family or friends outside the home." Now, that might sound a bit harsh, but one learns quickly, the music biz does not suffer fools. Arliss would allow me to get through about the first verse and chorus and then just stop me.

One day in late 1978, I called Arliss, and said I had a new song I wanted him to hear. Always the gracious one, he said, "Bring it on over." I took his Martin D-28 in my hands and I sang:

"All The Tea In China"

The rain outside my window~ Plays a sweet lullaby
But I can't sleep a wink tonight~ With you on my mind
So give me all the tea in China
A chalet in Carolina
And a piece of a peaceful Texas sky
And I will give it all up
Just to have you by my side
Oh what I would do
To be with you tonight
I thought love had a hold on you~ And I could tag along
Now I can't go my whole life through~ In this world alone
Repeat Chorus

"All The Tea In China"
Words & Music by Gary Owens ASCAP
United Artists/EMI Publishing

Before I finished singing the song, I knew Arliss liked it, based solely on the fact he hadn't stopped me midway through it. When the song ended he looked at me and said, "You've finally caught on to this song writing stuff."

Within a week, Arliss got me into LSI Recording Studios, on the tail end of a regular session. We cut "All The Tea In China." Among the great pickers on the session were Arliss on guitar and his brother Rick on drums. Rick Scott had just months prior, quit a group he had been a part of for the past five years in a club in Myrtle Beach. The club was "The Bowery." The group was "Alabama." Rick had co-written several of the bands songs that would go on to be big hits.

Six months after his leaving the group, Alabama members Randy, Jeff and Teddy had a new drummer and signed a recording contract with RCA. Harold Shedd was their producer. The rest is, as they say, music business history. I once told Rick: he and Pete Best (formerly of the Beatles) were the two most unluckiest drummers in the world.

Rick loved my new song and wanted to make the demo sound really great. We met at LSI Studio one day. Rick had asked Cajun singer Jo-El Sonnier to play concertina on my song, but after awhile Jo-El was the first to suggest the song didn't really call for that particular instrument.

I knew a kid who attended Belmont College named Gene Calvin. He was an all around genius. Gene didn't just play the violin. He allowed the most beautiful sounds to take wing from his fingertips through the strings. Now that's quite a statement to make, but with Gene it's more than appropriate. Gene was living, at the time, in a 1961 Chrysler, in the parking lot behind Mack's Country Cooking, where Broadway and Division meet at a point. Living with Gene, was his plump little girlfriend and their two, yes count'em, two dogs.

Rick called me early one cold morning and told me he could get us into the studio at ten that morning. He asked if I wanted my "fiddle player" friend to lay something down on my song. I said I would get in contact with Gene. It was around seven o'clock when I pulled up to Gene's car/home. I walked up and tapped on the frosty rear door glass. The window came down about an inch and a sleepy Gene greeted me. I quickly told him about the ten o'clock session at LSI and he said he'd be there.

As I left, I really didn't think he would make the session. At nine thirty, in walks Gene with his violin case. He took out his violin and tuned it. Arliss, Rick, and I, along with the engineer, sat in the control booth while Gene stood on the other side of the glass and listened to "All The Tea In China." Rick looked at me and asked, "Ain't he gonna chart it?" We all looked at each other with anticipation, as we had no idea how this might turn out.

After listening to the song one time Gene said, "Let's lay one down." More looks of anticipation. As the tape rolled Gene played the most beautiful violin part that sweetened the already beautiful melody. It added to the sense of loss and hurt ~ what the song was all about.

When Gene finished we all said, "Man that was great." Then Gene said, "I'd like to lay down a second part." We all readily agreed. Not having any idea how he would, or could improve on what he had just done, Gene then added a second track, which played off of, and answered to the first part to perfection. Gene then put his violin back in it's case and joined us in the control booth. We all sat and listened as the engineer played the final mix.

A few weeks later the song was released as a single on an independent label ~ Standing Stone Records. It was chosen as a Single Pick Hit in Billboard Magazine and got some airplay around the region. A friend named Allan Chapman, who was a staff writer with United Artists Music, at the time, the third largest music publisher in the world, played it for his boss, Jimmy Gilmer, president of United Artist's Nashville office.

Gilmer had been an artist with Dot Records, billed as Jimmy Gilmer and the Fireballs. He'd had two big hits, "Sugar Shack" in 1963 and "Bottle of Wine" in 1967. He liked my writing and my voice. He told me to hang around for a while, and I did hang around, for the most part of 1979.

I'd write a song. UA would pay for the demos and cut a check now and again to help me out. At this time, UA had a staff of 8 writers, of which only one, Richard Leigh, had experienced any success. He had a big hit with Crystal Gayle entitled "Don't It Make My Brown Eyes Blue?"

Buzz Arledge was working as the company's song plugger. That's the fella who goes out and plays the songs for producers and record people. Buzz and I became good friends and even co-wrote several songs. Buzz was also at that time, part of a duo known as "Martin and Arledge." He and his partner Hank Martin had a development deal with RCA Records. The great Norro Wilson was their producer.

It all seemed to be going well in my songwriting endeavors. I was working at the time as a night watchman at the Ramada Inn off Murfreesboro Road. My days were always free. I slept when I could. In December of 1979 Gilmer stuck his head into the tape copy room at UA and asked me, "How would you like to sign on as a staff writer?" I said "Sure!" On January 2nd of 1980 I signed a three year exclusive songwriting contract with United Artists.

I called my buddy Arliss and told him all about it and he said, "Well, so much for that five year plan huh?" I knew then. I was hooked.

Things started out good at UA. Oftentimes, after office hours, Gilmer would take us all to

Maude's Courtyard, a little place near Music Row, and we'd have drinks, eat boiled shrimp and sit and listen to Gilmer tell stories about the good old glory days of rock and roll. Gilmer was a great story teller. Sometimes we'd go to baseball games or hockey games.

I picked up extra income by singing cover songs for record labels sold exclusively in Europe. I sung a national jingle for "Maxell Tape." Thirty minutes work. It helped me live for a good long while.

As time went on, however, tensions began to surface. The writers were frustrated because the cuts weren't happening. Several complained about Buzz taking me to lunch too often and pitching my songs more frequently than theirs.

After a while, there was a lot of open animosity and of course, it could only get worse: which it did. When we writers got together and talked about the United Artists situation, it was always negative. I internalized everything. I allowed it to consume me. It was causing me to lay awake at night, grinding my teeth. My attitude got to be bad to the bone. I even turned away from my friend Buzz. Knowing all the while I was dead wrong, I destroyed just about all my relationships, turning away from friends and family. I even turned away from God. I am so thankful for the forgiving spirits of friends, family, and God. Without them, where would I be?

At one point, we thought things at UA had turned around. MGM purchased United Artists from Transamerica. There was going to be a big change coming down by way of new offices and better opportunities to get songs cut. Yes, it looked like happy days were here again. In a matter of just a few weeks, workers showed up and started building the new upstairs offices. It was exciting, until the other shoe dropped.

Enter Waylon Holyfield and Mark Wright, two highly successful writers who had left Welk Music to join the MGM/UA team. It didn't take long to realize: they *were* the team. The rest of us were development writers who hadn't quite panned out. Then came the facts concerning the whole UA sale.

United Artists Films had allowed some nitwit of a film director, named Michael Cimino to make a movie entitled, "Heaven's Gate." It was a long boring disaster at the box office, and it literally destroyed UA Films. Transamerica sold all UA holdings to MGM. All MGM wanted was the film catalog. They turned right around and sold the music publishing to CBS Music which finally ended up with EMI Music.

Somewhere in that spaghetti plate of multi million dollar deals were us little guys. We were small and the cracks were large. We all fell through. All of the writers except Leigh, Holyfield and Wright were dropped, as our contract options came around. It had been fun while it lasted.

The Death of Red Sovine

One day in 1980, I was on my way to visit a friend who lived on Lealand Avenue in Nashville. I was following a van along Harding Place. When the van reached the corner of Harding and Lealand, it suddenly went through the intersection, off the road, and into the yard of a corner house, where it hit a tree. I stopped, along with some others and ran into the yard approaching the driver's side. The driver was legendary Red Sovine: *(Figure 61)*.

Figure 61: Woodrow Wilson "Red" Sovine. Country music star. His recitations touched a lot of hearts.

He was dead. He had suffered a massive heart attack and probably had died before the collision with the tree. Red had been around in the music business a long time. He'd had many successful records, the most popular being "Teddy Bear."

Chapter 13

A Miracle

As of 1985, I had been a cigarette smoker for 26 years. I started out like a lot of kids my age, sneaking a cigarette from time to time, from my dad's pack on the sly. I had grown up in a society that promoted smoking. Even many of the educational films we were shown in elementary school were sponsored by "Old Gold" or "Chesterfield" cigarettes. It was only natural for a boy to one day become a bona fide smoker. It was almost a right of passage.

I had started out on "Camels." My father smoked "Lucky Strikes," so I was more or less weaned on non filtered cigarettes. I smoked those until I entered the Army. On my first day at boot camp, after running two miles, I was just about to die, but when the drill instructor said, "Smoke'em if you got'em," I lit up with all the others. A fellow soldier saw me lighting my Camel cigarette and said, "Man, those are going to kill you; here try one of these." He offered me a Marlboro. I stayed with that brand until I quit.

On December 16, 1985 I began to cough violently. Each time I coughed, there was blood. I was coughing up about a half ounce of blood every few minutes. I was rushed to Miller Clinic near my home. From there, Dr. David Bryant immediately sent me to Nashville's West Side Hospital. The doctors performed a bronchoscopy and discovered my left lung was full of blood, and it was beginning to overflow into my right lung. Once again in my life, I was drowning. I was admitted and set up with medication to slow my heart rate. I was scheduled for surgery the following morning. They were going to remove my left lung.

A friend had called my family in Illinois. Later in the evening my hospital room was full of family and friends. I was heavily medicated, and I was fading in and out.

Sometime later that night, after the visitors had gone, my sister Sandra (Sis) came into my room and woke me. She had with her a piece of a Ritz cracker; a small cup of grape juice, and a small vial of oil. She gave me communion with the cracker and juice. She then rubbed the oil on my forehead and began to pray. As she prayed, she would at times speak in tongues. I lay there thinking of only one thing in my medicated state. I believed with all my heart: what she was doing would work. This was a big step for me, as I had for many years mocked and criticized Sis for her strong faith. Though I had been saved and baptized at age ten, many years of backsliding had turned me into quite a heathen. At five A.M., the doctors came into my room and told me they wanted to take another look into my left lung. If some of the blood had receded, perhaps they could save a portion of the lung. They conducted their exam and then rolled me back to my room, where my family had gathered to wait out the operation.

Three doctors stood in my hospital room at West Side Hospital on December 17th, 1985 and proclaimed: not only was there *no blood* in my lungs, they were unable to find any cause for the bleeding. They were baffled. I told them about my sister; about the prayer. One of them said, "If it wasn't for God's intervention, we doctors wouldn't have nearly the success rate." I never smoked another cigarette.

A Prison Ministry

I had just gone through the ordeal with my lungs and had stopped smoking. I had also re-evaluated my life ~ my priorities. I wanted to get out of Nashville. My songwriting career was in the toilet, and I had grown bitter and weary of all the politics, and the insincerity plaguing the business.

I moved to Atlanta, Georgia and got a job as a church custodian at the Clarkston Baptist Church, in nearby Clarkston. The night before I applied for the job, a group of deacons had gone to the home of the Pastor of the church, where they confronted him with a question. They asked this 57 year old man, who had been their spiritual leader for the past 16 years, if he had been having sex with a 13 year old mentally impaired boy, the son of church members, in his church office. He answered "Yes!" They accepted his resignation then and there. The 1800 church members were split right down the middle. The older folks refused to believe the pastor would do such a thing, even though he had owned up to it. The other half wanted to not only fire him but lynch him as well.

The church, without a full time pastor, was vulnerable. Without strong leadership, it was flying by the seat of its pants and committees clashed over decisions involving church policy and finances. Sunday services were conducted by pinch hitters, whose strengths didn't lie in the pulpit.

One Sunday, the music minister preached, the following Sunday, the youth pastor went at it. Then various members who taught Sunday school classes took a turn. All the while, a search committee was working frantically to find a special someone with ~ the gift. Someone who could come in and pick up the pieces and make the church whole again.

Clarkston Baptist Church found that in Steve Hammack. Steve was young, with a beautiful dedicated wife, and two precious children. Soon the church was back on track.

Each Wednesday morning, the staff of eight people would meet in the Pastor's Study for a devotional. We would open with a prayer, and a different staff member would do something special. Some would read a scripture, while another would perhaps share a testimony. I was still writing songs. Now they were Christian oriented. I had yet to share them with anyone, so when my turn to conduct a devotional came around, I took my guitar with me, and shared a song I had recently written.

Ordinary People

When your trials and troubles
Begin to mount
Remember with the Lord at your side
The odds don't even count
    Ain't it amazing ~ ain't it great
    How He gives His sweet loving Grace

He's Using Ordinary People~In Everyday Ways
To reach the people~Who've lost their way
Spread the Word~Have you heard~Jesus saves
Using Ordinary People in everyday ways

He can part the water
Change it to wine
Touch the hearts of the poor lost souls
And change their lives
    Ain't it amazing ~ and not too late
    You can have His sweet loving Grace

"Ordinary People"
Words & Music written by Gary Owens ASCAP
Copyright Siler Creek Music ASCAP

When I finished, Steve asked if I would sing the song at the next Sunday service. That Sunday night I sang "Ordinary People" in a church packed with around 600 members. I was terribly nervous. I had, by this time, been singing in public for years but, it had been in dark noisy bars, singing for drunks, with a four piece band behind me.

As Steve got up to introduce me I said a quiet simple prayer; "Lord, please keep me from messing up." No sooner had I finished the prayer, than a peaceful thought came to my mind. I sincerely believe it was an answer to my little prayer. It was as though an inaudible voice said, "Gary, this is Jesus, I'll be sitting in the back row. Look over the heads of all these people and sing to me." When Steve finished introducing me, I calmly walked up front, sat down with my guitar and sang better than I had ever sung in my life.

A few days later, an assistant to the music minister, a fellow named Dan Feldman, called me. He had a friend who did prison ministry. He and another man went around to the various state prisons throughout Georgia. He suggested I meet him. Dan's friend was Henry Williams. He was sixty-seven years old; blind in one eye. The detail of the eye is pertinent to the story, only because Henry was teamed up with a blind preacher named Jessie Moore. Jessie was a 53 year old black man of the cloth. He could make the rafters shake when he got to preaching. Henry would drive Jessie to the prisons throughout Georgia, and Jessie would preach. After I joined the team: *(Figure 62)* and we had made a few weekend trips together, I felt comfortable enough to kid them about how, with Jessie being totally blind and Henry blind in one eye, we could bill ourselves as "The Three Guys With Three Eyes." They thought it was pretty funny.

Figure 62: Here I am with Bros. Henry Williams (center) and Jessie Moore (right) on the beach at Savannah, Georgia.

On Saturday afternoons, I would meet Henry at his home. We would drive to Griffin, Georgia, and pick up Brother Jessie. We then traveled to whatever part of the state the prison was located. Occasionally we'd go to a prison close by, but most required long driving and overnight stays.

216

Upon our arrival at a prison we were subjected to a search: then once we got into the chapel, which was usually a cafeteria, I would sing three songs and Brother Jessie would preach. He preached the same sermon on each trip. I learned it by heart.

He would start out kind of soft and slow, telling how he had been feeling "Kinda poorly lately." So he went to see Doctor Law, and he told the doctor how, "My feets are sick, they's always wantin' to walk into sinful places like them juke joints!" He would continue with, "And Doctor Law, my arms are feelin' poorly, you see, they's always reachin' out to hold another man's wife!" With each step of the sermon, he would get louder, and the prisoners, especially the blacks, would begin to talk back with "preach on brother" and the likes.

While dealing with Doctor Law, it became obvious, there would be no treatment. No healing. Only condemnation and death. At this point, the prisoners would be emotionally involved with the service. Brother Jessie would kick it up a notch and tell how he came to realize Doctor Law could not help him, so he went "Down the hall a ways and entered the office of Doctor Grace."Now there were signs of forgiveness, hope, and healing, and all the promises God made to man when Jesus died for his sins.

We would end the service with a song of invitation. We would then visit with the prisoners for awhile. Some would just come up and tell us they enjoyed the service. Occasionally, one would walk up and start telling how he had just been transformed by the service. Then he'd ask if he could have a phone number to contact us.

I learned, rather quickly, the con games prisoners play on anyone unaware. They can be quite manipulative. They will call and ask for ridiculous favors like, "Would you write a letter to the parole board attesting to the fact I'm a changed man and should be released?" Although Marion Federal Prison had taught me a lot about these characters, I let my guard down, though briefly, but I soon made a commitment to myself. If I was going to continue with Bros. Henry and Jessie, I could not go jumping through hoops for a bunch of convicts.

On one of our trips, I asked Jessie if he had been born blind. He told me how he had started having problems with his eyesight at age 14, and it just got worse. At some point he had gotten involved with a clinic for the blind in Atlanta, but he was trying hard to maintain his independence, though at the time his vision was faint and blurred.

One day, in 1953, at the age of 19, Jessie was rounding a corner in downtown Atlanta. He ran square into a white woman, knocking her to the sidewalk, then tumbled down on top of her with her screaming bloody murder. Jessie, all bewildered, was just trying to get untangled from the situation. He told how several white men grabbed him and commenced to beat on him, as the woman continued screaming. They were hitting him over and over calling him "nigger," with every other expletive one could think of.

Soon the police arrived. However, they were not there to rescue Brother Jessie but to arrest him. They handcuffed him, then roughed him up on the way to the police station. Remember, this was Atlanta, Georgia, America ~ in the year 1953.

So there sat Jessie in jail. He had been there several days when his counselor from the blind clinic heard about the situation. The gentleman got Jessie out of jail and went through a lot of bureaucratic red tape to have the charges dropped.

He told Jessie it was time to start accepting the fact ~ he was going blind. When navigating the streets of Atlanta, he needed to send out the message: "Hey I'm blind. I can't see you, so you watch out for me!" From then on he started using a white tipped cane and wearing dark glasses. By the time I met Brother Jessie, he was totally blind.

Our sojourns paid no money. Henry footed the bill for everything. Gas, rooms, and meals. I recall how each time we dropped Bro. Jessie off at his home, Henry would slip him some money. Jessie worked part time for Griffin Industries, sorting nuts and bolts, but he was still poor. Occasionally Henry would get us into a church to procure a love offering, in which all the money taken up went to Bro. Jessie. Henry worked for the state of Georgia and I was making a living, so we agreed ~ the "love offerings" would go to Bro. Jessie.

The churches were always "black churches." I don't intend to stereotype, but I think most black folks will agree ~ they like their worship services very long, very loud, and feverish. Before Bro. Jessie preached, I would sit down with my guitar and sing my three songs. The folks were always appreciative, and although my style of music was different from theirs, I always received a thunderous response. Bro. Jessie's style of preaching, on the other hand, was right up their alley.

One such service went on for hours. Jessie preached, of course, the sermon on Doctors Law & Grace. The congregation joined in with shouts of encouragement, as an organist played jazzy little riffs to enhance and punctuate the message.

On this occasion, following the sermon, the church's pastor got up and announced they would be taking up a "love offering." As the organist fingered the keys, the pastor yelled out, "Twenty dollar givers come on down!" Folks, looking like the cast from "Porgy and Bess," left their pews, strutting down front, peeling double sawbucks from thick green wads; dropping the bills into the plate. Then: "Ten dollar givers come on down!" On and on through the "Five dollar givers," and "One dollar givers." Then in an excited manner the Pastor jumped around screaming "Little children, pocket change, pocket change!!!" The service ended with a long hard driving song with much hand clapping, jumping, dancing, arms up, praising God. At one point, a little old grandmother behind me who was dancing and jumping around cried out, *"If Jesus comes through the roof, I'll pay for the shingles!!"*

I continued with Bros. Henry and Jessie for three more years until, due to job scheduling, I had to give it up. It had been a joy spending time on the road with them, and I have many fond memories of all the places we went, and the people we met.

Does God Really Need A Con Man?

I got sidetracked for a while by working with another prison ministry in Decatur, Georgia. The man who headed it up had, at one time, been a con man, pimp, and hustler. We would go to prisons and churches together. I would sing. He would preach.

He always injected into his sermons, a line about, "I used to be a con man and a hustler and well, I still am, but now I'm conning and hustling for the Lord." One day I asked him, "Does God really need a con man out there working for him?" His reply was, "Hey, it works for me!" The prison ministry was a sham. There were many good people used in the course of it's work, but most were unaware of it's leader's true nature. For the most part it was just smoke and mirrors designed to get money from unsuspecting Christians who thought their giving would be helping convicts or their families. The money only supported this man's lifestyle.

Back at the office, men and women would often walk in off the street having been just released from jail or prison. Upon their release from prison, they were given one pair of khaki pants, a white shirt, black work boots and $25. They were usually hungry and lost as to where to go and what to do next. Most had no family nearby. Many had burned all their bridges.

I made a list of companies willing to hire ex-convicts. Soon, I was sending guys to Consolidated Freight or Bowman Trucking and others. The work was hard, but it paid good and it was a new beginning for them. I would set up bus schedules for them and even provide a bus pass, good for a week. They could travel around Atlanta unlimited.

I joined Second Harvest Food Bank. Then, I started a food pantry. Instead of going around to churches begging for food and getting petty amounts of can goods, I would call a church and explain how, by being a member of Second Harvest, I could buy food for ten cents a pound. I told them I didn't want canned goods. I needed money! I would go to Second Harvest with fifty dollars and get five hundred pounds of food. That's a lot of food to pass out to folks who have none. The boss man would sometimes load up his car with groceries to take home. Second Harvest's rules for membership stated: parties involved with distributing food could not benefit from it. The boss man hated that.

Another job put on me was: Assistant Chaplain of the DeKalb County Jail. With over 1200 inmates behind bars at any given time, there were many occasions, at least once a month, when a prisoner's immediate family member would pass away. It was my job to inform the prisoner. The jail would call me, always at a late hour. No matter what time of day the jail received the death notice, they always waited until the prisoners were locked in and asleep. It reduced the possibility of dealing with a distraught inmate and having other prisoners get worked up. I would go to the jail, and wait in a small cinder block room with a desk and a phone. A jailer would bring the prisoner in. Most knew a meeting of this kind meant only one thing. A death in the family.

Many times the prisoner would be anxious. Sometimes indifferent. If the prisoner wanted to make a phone call, I would arrange it. If he desired to attend the funeral, I made those arrangements.

If the prisoner opted for the funeral, he would be accompanied by two guards and myself. We would enter with the prisoner through a side door. He would be dressed in a bright orange jump suit with the big letters D.C.J on the back. He would be handcuffed to a wide leather belt wrapped around his waist. A chain ran from the belt to the leg irons

223

on his ankles. There, before all the family and friends of the deceased, he would either maintain his composure, or lose it. Either way, we were in and out in a matter of minutes. Then, for the prisoner, it was back to the routine of doing time.

I was sickened by the man who ran this racket, calling it a prison ministry. One morning, an investigator with the Georgia Department of Corrections came by and started asking questions about my boss. It seems a list of names of people who regularly visited Georgia State Prisons was entered into a computer. The computer then spit back out several names with the question, "Why are these people allowed into the prisons?" My boss' name was on that list.

I answered the man's questions, saying nothing damaging. After all, my personal opinion was all I had against the guy. However, after I complied with the investigation on him, he called me into his office, demanding to know what was asked of me and how I had replied. I told him I could not say. I had been instructed not to reveal any aspect of the investigation. I then advised him I would clear out my office within the hour. I had been ready to leave the job for quite a while. Less than 10 minutes later ~ I was gone.

Stained Glass

I admit I was a malcontent. I was still trying to find my niche in life. So far, the quest had been elusive. Someone once said, "Find something you can make a living at, something you really enjoy doing, and you'll never have to work a day." That's what I was looking for. I had never been afraid of hard work, but futile labor for the sake of mere survival made that survival much less meaningful.

One day I picked up a copy of Entrepreneur Magazine and was encouraged to find there was actually a publication directed at people like me. After looking into some of the opportunities available, I realized one must have what is called start up money. I kept my eyes open. I knew there was something out there, just right for me.

I discovered stained glass! I had often admired it, with no thought of how it was created. One day I was in a mall and there was a stained glass shop with a sign reading "Sign up now for classes." I did just that.

It wasn't like I was going to Harvard or anything. The classes consisted of three weeks: two nights per week. It was painless, and when I finished I knew all I needed to know about stained glass. All I knew were the basics. The bare basics. Over the next two years I would make many projects, some of which I'd like to hunt down today and destroy. But, I kept at it.

I was getting better with each project. Over a period of several months I created about 30 stained glass panels, each one framed in wood and fitted with chain for hanging. Each piece was around 18" by 24" and consisted of varying subject matter. There were birds, flowers, angels, and much more. With my gaining more skill came a greater degree of difficulty; the greater number of pieces, the more intricate the cuts. I learned to choose the perfect piece of glass for a project. It became second nature.

I had heard about a large flea market in Ringgold, Georgia and drove up to check it out. An indoor mall had gone belly up, then converted into a flea market. According to friends, who had visited there, it was packed, one weekend a month.

I signed up for a 12' by 12' booth and began to put my presentation together. On a Thursday night, I drove up with my stained glass panels and set them up in the designated area. Friday was slow. All agreed, Fridays were always slow. Saturday and Sunday would be the big days.

To the right of my booth, was a fellow who had several antique beds and quite a few rifles and shotguns. The stuff was topnotch. To my left, was a guy who looked like something right out of "Deliverance." He had brought in a literal truckload of stuff. The kind of items you see at yard sales.

The flea market drew thousands of people, and each person who came through my space went on and on about how beautiful each piece was.

Although my prices were well below that of comparable stained glass pieces, no one was buying. It was the same for the bed and gun merchant next to me. Not one sell.

Mr. "Deliverance," on the other hand, would sit back with his straw cowboy hat pulled down over his eyes and every few minutes someone would pick up an item and ask, "How much do you want for this?" He would take a gander at it, and say in his slow southern accent, "I gotta have a dolluh for that." That's all we heard the entire weekend. "How much?" and "Gotta have a dolluh!"

One local told me how the "junk man" was a well known character in the area. He would go around hitting all the yard sales and could also be seen, on occasions, picking through the city dump.

They say one man's trash is another man's treasure. When all was said and done, I had sold nothing. The bed & gun guy made zip, zero! The junk man took in over $800 in cash.

After that, I started just giving the stained glass away. When someone admired a particular piece, and I knew they probably couldn't afford it, I would surprise them with, "Here, I want you to have it." I received more enjoyment in doing that than I would have had I sold them. The one main benefit in my discovering stained glass was: it set me in line to meet one of the most interesting and likable persons I've ever known. Derek Christopher Anthony Buffardi.

Our first meeting was not a pleasant one, and it was all my doing. I had seen an advertisement, for colored nuggets, from a stained glass supply company outside of Atlanta known as "Jennifer's Stained Glass." It was the premier supplier for most of the southeast United States. I drove there one hot miserable day ~ in a van with no air conditioning. I was having a bad day overall. When I arrived, I was already in a foul mood. I walked in and was informed they were out of what I had come for.

I blew my Irish top. I went storming out, cussing like a sailor. Following me out to my van was the fella who had been the victim of my tirade. He had about him, a calm and cool countenance. Amid all my anger he said, "Hey man, I don't wanna fight you, I just wanna sell you something." He shamed me. Had it been possible, I would have crawled under a rock.

I felt the anger leave me. We became instant friends and remain so to this day. He still has that kind, calming spirit toward his fellow man. He and his beautiful wife Martha, along with their two sons, live in Kennesaw, Georgia. I will always consider them ~ my friends!

Inspiration

In the past I had always been good at catching a song idea. Songwriters must always have their "antennae" up, so to speak. I must admit though, before one particular evening I had never been hit with an idea that seemed to write itself. It's nearly a religious experience.

I was visiting in Illinois in 1989 over the Christmas holidays, and at my sister's urging, I went to visit my Aunt Margaret. My Uncle Carl had passed away recently, and Aunt Margaret was still mourning. During our visit, she mentioned something about a plant my uncle had set out on the fence line of the next door neighbor. The neighbors had given him so much grief over the plant, my aunt felt as though it had contributed to his demise.

Later, as I was driving from her home I started thinking about what my aunt had mentioned, concerning the plant by the fence. I was overwhelmed with a song idea. Along Interstate 57, between Marion and Bonnie, Illinois, the words and melody came so effortlessly to me.

By the time I got to my mother's home, it was written. I grabbed a pencil and legal pad, and scribbled it down before I could forget any part of it. Then, I picked up my guitar and sang the song.

"My Neighbor's Vine"

Neighbor John put a plant in the ground out by the fence
That stood between his place and mine
From it came a rosebud I knew was Heaven sent
It grew over onto my yard in time.

I never said a word like some I know who would
For the beauty of the roses was sublime
Through the years they grew ~ set against a sky of blue
And I thanked God for My Neighbor's Vine

Chorus: It takes God's love to make the roses grow
Crossing over where people draw the line
I beheld the beauty of the rose like it was mine
And I thanked God for My Neighbor's Vine

Neighbor John since passed away and I've heard people say
His life was just a cup of bitter wine
But I still like to think of the beauty he displayed
With the roses in his yard and mine

When it rains you know it rains on the good and bad alike
Soaking the land through and through
And when the sun comes out from behind the darkest cloud
It shines down on the likes of me and you

Repeat Chorus

"My Neighbor's Vine"
Words & Music written by Gary Owens ASCAP
Copyright Marledge Music Inc ASCAP

Orchids In The Snow

While in Illinois, I had gotten acquainted with a couple in the city of Mount Vernon. Steve and Kathy Allen. They had started a ministry from out of their home and were as dedicated as any I had ever seen. They knew I had some experience in prison ministry, so they wanted me to stay in Illinois and work with them. My life was so screwed up. I was afraid to make any kind of major decisions, as I had made so many mistakes already. I spent an entire day at their home, as they tried to convince me to stay and work with them.

In the end, I decided to return to Georgia. The day before I left, it had snowed quite a lot, but I made one last trip out to see Steve and Kathy. I took with me, a gift. A beautiful stained glass panel of Orchids. It was my most prized piece. I wanted them to have it. When I arrived and presented the panel to them, Steve set it in a window to let the bright sunshine come through. Kathy left the room and soon returned with a book of devotions she had been reading. In it was a passage. *"You shall know him by the orchids in the snow."* I was a bit spooked by the passage and was tempted to stay, but I did go. Anywhere else was still preferable to southern Illinois.

Chapter 14

Hello Georgia Goodbye

When I got back to Georgia, I started stockpiling money. I was working on a loading dock for Consolidated Freight, the same company where I had sent ex-convicts for jobs. It was slave labor. No matter how hard we worked, they still yelled at us about not working hard enough. The fact was, they kept my name on the call sheet ~ evidence I was cutting it.

I received a letter one day from my old buddy Buzz Arledge, from the United Artist days. He had started his own publishing company, Marledge Music and had been having some success with songs like "Dear Me" recorded by Lorrie Morgan and "Holdin' a Good Hand" by Lee Greenwood. He had sent me a song transfer agreement on a tune I had written years earlier. I signed it and mailed it back, and sometime later we spoke on the phone.

It was good to hear Buzz's voice. During our conversation, he asked if I was doing any writing. I told him I had written a few new things. He wanted to hear them. I sent him a copy of "My Neighbor's Vine." Buzz called a few days later and encouraged me to give Nashville another try.

Nashville II

I returned to Nashville with a whole new attitude toward the music business. I found an apartment in the Belmont section of town. It was a one bedroom, with knotty pine walls, hardwood floors, and a stone fireplace. It could have just as well been a cabin in the mountains. I secured a job. A short time later I signed with Marledge Music as a staff writer.

I had changed as a writer. I knew the business had changed as well. The first being a good thing. The latter: not so good. I began to build my catalog with Marledge Music. At least once a month, we would schedule a session, and I would have at least four new songs to offer up. Buzz would book the best studios. Buzz's great production skills, along with top drawer pickers, insured my songs always came out sounding like hits.

Response to my music was positive, however Nashville is full of great writers and the competition is fierce. I was having my songs put on a hold status by artists and producers, and I had several songs recorded by new artists who were shopping record deals with the major labels. It was a good indicator. We were doing something right. When you think of the monumental odds against having a song recorded, it can become quite discouraging. A record label preparing an album project will hear perhaps a couple thousand songs. The record label's A&R people are listening, as well as the producers, and artists. To go through all those tunes and end up with 10 for an album, means an awful lot of great songs had to fall by the wayside.

The big cuts weren't forthcoming, but I still felt good about my songs. Other accomplished writers were supportive of my works. I had learned to tell the difference between the smoke blowing B.S. artists and the sincere people. I respected the opinions of a few select songwriters, as well as Buzz and a fellow named Jimmy Darrell. Jimmy had been in the business for many years. He had, at one time, been the head man in Mel Tillis' organization. He really knew his stuff. Buzz and I respected Jimmy a lot, and we both appreciated his good counsel.

I was just happy to have a publisher, a home base to operate out of. What, with working a full time job and my monthly draw against future royalties, I was paying my way.

I started attending a church in nearby Franklin, Tennessee. There I met a wonderful lady named Dorothy. She kept me well grounded, in contrast to the whimsical music business. She made me feel good about myself, independent of the music. As time went on we began to plan our lives together. In 1994 we married.

A New New Beginning

Buzz and I both grew weary of the music business. The politics had become more complex, and the record companies had closed ranks to shut out the average songwriter. By this time I was focused more on my new family, our home and just making a living.

Buzz gave up his office at Fireside Studios, keeping the publishing company in name only. He began a new career in teaching and did so until health problems began to interfere. He was diagnosed with Multiple Sclerosis and has since been involved with ongoing treatments, as well as a major surgery. Buzz and I still go down to Music Row from time to time, to pitch songs, but we no longer take the business so serious. The most positive thing about Buzz and me putting the music business aside: it allowed our friendship to exist without the stress of a professional relationship.

In the music industry, the powers that be can smell desperation. If a writer does not apply himself with a do or die attitude, it's impossible to establish a reputable career. I sometimes listen to my song catalog, and I am proud of my works. All in all I look back and consider the breaks I had, and chances to do better in the business. I have to sum it all up with this simple evaluation: In a nutshell, I never wanted it bad enough, and I can live with it.

A Friend Says Goodbye

Our dear friend Fay Dickinson began to show signs of poor health. Sometime in 1994, she had to be moved to a nursing facility. Each Sunday after church, Dorothy and I would visit her. She still had the most wonderful attitude about life. From Fay's room window, one could see the high rise where she had lived for years ~ the Wessex Towers. It made her new living arrangement so much more sad, perhaps more so for her visitors than Fay.

Over the years, Fay had always encouraged me in my songwriting, and then in 1995, Ricky Skaggs recorded one of my songs entitled "Solid Ground." It was the title of the album, as well as the first single. Fay was so happy for me. I believe she got more joy out of it than anyone. I had written a song for my wife entitled "With You." Fay loved the song. Of all I had written, it was her favorite.

One night we went to see Fay, as we knew the end was near. We entered her room to the sound of a beeping monitor along with little flashing lights registering the life still remaining. We sat at her bedside. An attending nurse told us Fay was not conscious of her surroundings, yet as I held her hand and began to quietly sang "With You," she squeezed my hand.

"With You"

If I were a seashell down by the sea shore
and you came along
You'd pick me up and listen close
Then you'd take me home
   There I'd be whenever you might need
   a warm summer breeze blowing through
   It's not much but you see
   At least I'd get to be, With You.

If I were a flower growing in the wild
And one day you reached down
I'd spend my days in the pages of a book
Where your secret thoughts are found
   I'll be that songbird singing in a tree
   In the park when you come strolling through
   It's not much but you see
   at least I'd get to be , With You.

I know I'll, I'll never feel the touch of your hand
But every night in my dreams I'll be with you any way I can

   I'll be that butterfly catching your eye
   on a lazy afternoon with nothing to do
   It's not much but you see
   At least I'd get to be, With You

"With You"
Words & Music written by Gary Owens ASCAP
Copyright Marledge Music Publishing Inc ASCAP

237

We stayed for a while longer, then left. We had no idea the end would come so quickly. Only minutes after arriving home, we received a call from our friend, Mary Ann Hoffmann, Fay's longtime friend. Fay was gone.

Fay had donated her body to the Vanderbilt School of Medicine for research in diabetes, so there was no funeral. A couple months later Mary Ann called to tell us Fay's daughter, Beth, an attorney in upstate New York, was coming down to hold a memorial service. Mary asked if I would do something special for the occasion. I sat down that afternoon and wrote a song about my dear friend, Fay Dickinson ~ champion to many. It was entitled "That Kind Of Love."

One special evening in late autumn, a great number of people gathered in the Pineapple Room of Cheekwood's Tennessee Botanical Gardens and paid tribute to this special human being. There were those who, each in turn, stepped up to the podium and shared precious memories of their dear friend. A few days earlier I had gone into a studio and recorded "That Kind Of Love". During the service I played it over a sound system, as I knew emotionally I could not sing it live.

"That Kind Of Love"

She made life look so easy
Everyday show some kindness for another
And I am convinced ~ she was Heaven sent
Solely for the sake of others

Always a smile on her sweet face
Down that last mile right through her final days
Where she once stood now stands an empty place
But she left love on all she touched along the way

With that kind of love ~ we can move mountains
With that kind of love ~ we can roll away the stone
And it will be done with the help that comes from God above
Lord please fill our hearts with That Kind Of Love

All good things come from Heaven
And for a while they're our very own
Now the Good Lord gives and the Good Lord takes
He sent angels to carry her home

Repeat Chorus

"That Kind Of Love"
Words & Music written by Gary Owens ASCAP
Copyright Siler Creek Music ASCAP

Following the memorial service, Fay's daughter and Grandchildren with about two dozen of Fay's friends, gathered at Ruth's Chris Steak Restaurant on Nashville's West End. We had a wonderful dinner: a get-together Fay had planned months before her death, as well as having provided the funds. We ate, drank, laughed, and shared the most fondest memories of our special friend. The bill for the night was well over three thousand dollars.

It was just the kind of evening Fay would have enjoyed and I truly believe she did!

Other Heroes

Having been involved with the music business for many years, I have had dealings with "celebrities." There are three people in the "Star" end of the business whom I hold in high regard ~ Connie Smith, Eddy Arnold, and Sheb Wooley.

Connie Smith: *(Figure 63)* and I were introduced by a mutual friend, Milton Blackford. We tried to co~write a song or two. She had just signed with Warner Bros. Records and was working on rekindling her career after taking off several years to raise her children. Nothing resulted from our venture, but it was an honor to be in the presence of this beautiful lady. Sometime later she married singer Marty Stuart and continues to appear on the Grand Ole Opry as well as other venues. She is a real born again lady, and she's always been my all time favorite female singer.

Figure 63: Connie Smith. A real lady. My all time favorite lady singer.

I met Eddy Arnold: *(Figure 64)* in 1995. I had dropped off a demo of my song "With You" at his office in Brentwood. Later that day he called me at home, to tell me he loved the song and wanted to put it on his next album. I would drop by his office from time to time and we would have great visits, discussing everything from politics to life in general. He respected, a great deal, the late Illinois Senator Everett Dirksen. Luckily I had a few Everett Dirksen stories tucked away from my growing up in Illinois, during his time in office.

Figure 64: Eddy Arnold. The man who brought country music to a respectable level.

Eddy would pick up his guitar and sing "With You," and I was thrilled to hear that trademark "Eddy Arnold" voice singing my song. Time went by and the project never materialized. Then, a short while later Eddy retired. The music business will always be a business of close calls and near misses.

Eddy passed away on May 8, 2008, two months after the death of his beloved wife, Sally.

My old buddy Sheb Wooley: *(Figure 65)* passed away on September 16, 2003. It wasn't unexpected, as he had been dealing with leukemia for quite a while. He was having good days and bad days. He had just returned home from Johnny Cash's wake, when according to his wife Linda, he just sat down and died. Sheb had done it all. He was the writer, and artist, who had a monster hit in 1958 entitled "Purple People Eater" and later "That's My Pa." He had a string of parody hits as his alter ego, "Ben Colder," as well as writing the theme song for TVs "Hee Haw." He had starred on TVs "Rawhide" as scout "Pete Nolan" and was in about 70 motion pictures, including "High Noon", "Giant', and "Hoosiers."

Figure 65: My Old buddy Sheb Wooley (L) with Eric Fleming and Clint Eastwood on TVs "Rawhide."

243

Sheb and I wrote about ten songs together, and just being around him was a joy. Every time we went to lunch at the Mason Jar, a little meat and three in Hendersonville, I had to fight him for the check. I once told him how he had always been a hero of mine. I think it pleased him. He was one of the most generous, giving, and talented human beings I ever knew.

A few years earlier, in 1983, Linda Dotson, Sheb's wife and manager, had called me about a friend they had out in Beverly Hills, California, who was looking for a country songwriter to co-write with. His name was Bob Merrill: *(Figure 66)*. Linda went on to explain how Bob had been successful in the past, but hadn't written in quite a while.

Figure 66: Songwriter /Composer Bob Merrill.

He had written "How Much is That Doggie in the Window." It had been a big hit for Patti Page.
He also wrote, "If I Knew You Were Comin' I'd've Baked a Cake," as well as "Honeycomb" by Jimmie

Rodgers. Then, she hit me with the real show stoppers. He had written "People" which Barbara Streisand had performed in "Funny Girl." It had been a big hit single as well. He had also written the music for the Broadway hit, "Carnival."

I gave Bob a call. We talked for quite a while and touched on a couple ideas. Then, one day we spent about two hours on a song idea. We were both pretty excited about it.

Bob was 64 years old at the time and was having some health problems. The song project was put on hold. We talked from time to time. Then I moved to Atlanta and lost contact with him.

One day in 1998, after growing more ill, Bob left his Beverly Hills mansion and drove to nearby Culver City, a Los Angeles suburb. While sitting alone in his car, he shot himself. His wife Suzanne stated: "He didn't want to spend the rest of his life in a wheelchair."

A Hollywood Connection

When I was 12 years old, I sent one of my poems to an outfit in Hollywood called "Buddy Bregman Productions." They had ads: *(Figure 67)* in the back of most every magazine published in those days. I received a contract from them offering to put music to my words for the fee of $59 ~ a magnificent sum to a 12 year old in 1963. Sending a couple dollars at a time, it took me a year to pay it off. Soon I received the sheet music and was so proud to see where it read "Beautiful Attraction," words by Gary Owens, music by Buddy Bregman. My first collaboration.

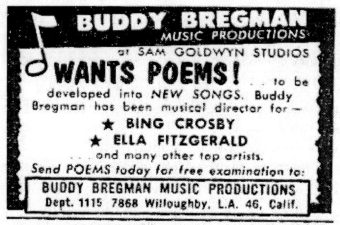

Figure 67: This ad was in every magazine in the 1950s. It gave many young budding songwriters a chance to test their talent.

A few weeks later, some friends and I were at a theater to see a Jerry Lewis movie called "The Delicate Delinquent." It was Lewis' first film since breaking off from partner Dean Martin. In the opening credits, in huge letters, it read, Music by Buddy Bregman. I felt like I was in great company.

The point to all of this is: one day in 2007 I spoke with Buddy Bregman on the phone. During our conversation Buddy told me Bob Merrill was his uncle. It really is a small world.

A Pair Of Shoes

We seldom know the who, what, when, where or why of life's comings and goings ~ unaware of how our touch may affect the lives of others.

The first day of school will always be a big day for kids. Seeing old friends; making new ones. I remember it as a day when the broadest line was unintentionally drawn between the have and have not. There were those on the first day who came with the 500 sheet tablet, a mess of pencils, and the super duper, triple decker box of crayons, with a built in sharpener ~ while others showed up with the modest 25 sheet pack, a couple pencils and the economy box of 8 crayons. I was of the latter. My parents weren't poor, but at the same time, with four children, they had to be pretty frugal.

One's attire was the main point of interest on that first day. Just about every kid showed up in brand new clothes. Boys were more obvious, by virtue of the undeniable newness of wrangler jeans and brand spanking new black leather shoes.

The year was 1958. Fourth grade. First day. Valier Grade School. Among the aforementioned, sat Johnny Newberry: (Figure 68). He was wearing a dull dingy T-shirt, worn-out frazzled jeans with holes in the knees, and his feet were bare. In those days, Johnny's family, like a lot of families in southern Illinois, were known as *reliefers* ~ nowadays called welfare recipients.

Johnny's father, Coy Newberry, was an alcoholic, and his drunken antics kept Johnny supplied with many a funny story. Yet, behind the facade, it was obvious this family of nine lacked and suffered with their lot in life.

Figure 68: Johnny Newberry. His freshman year in high school. 1963

I shall never forget the sadness I felt when I saw Johnny sitting there, with a broad smile on his face, so happy to be back in school. His teeth were rotting out at such a young age. I suppose in his world, in those innocent times, he was ignorant of any fear of embarrassment or shame.

I could hardly wait till school let out that first day. I rushed home and told my mother about Johnny. She asked me if there was something I wanted to do about it. I told her I wanted to give

Johnny my Sunday shoes. She agreed. I ran to my room and got the shoes. Mom drove me to Valier, and we stopped in front of the Newberry's dilapidated unpainted shanty. I ran to the front porch and placed the shoes by the door. I knocked on the door and ran back to the car. My mother and I made our getaway. The next day at school, there sat Johnny Newberry wearing those nice shiny black shoes. He seemed so happy, and I was happy for him.

Fast forward now, to the year 1976. 18 years had passed. I was working in a factory in Herrin, Illinois, and after work one evening I stopped off at a tavern called the Rome Club. Sitting at the bar, nursing a beer, was Johnny Newberry. It had been nearly ten years since our high school graduation. It had been that long since I had seen him. Johnny had served in the military and in that time Uncle Sam had provided him with pearly white dentures. He was neatly dressed. He had a good job. He had really come a long way. We started talking about the "good old days" and at one point he said, "I knew it was you who gave me those shoes." I was startled, as it came from out of no where. I asked, "Why didn't you say something back then?" He kind of shrugged and said, "Oh, I didn't want to embarrass you." It was the last time I saw Johnny. On October 29, 1983, as he drove to work, Johnny Newberry was killed by a drunk driver.

Epilogue

It is said, "When we remember a time, we remember moments." I hope this book will give my children, and theirs, a record of some *moments* from my life.   Hopefully they will avoid many of my mistakes. Because it was intended for them, I have left much out. There's just an awful lot about my life I wouldn't want my children to know.

My mother has a story about me, from when I was three years old. At the time, we were living in Peoria, Illinois, in an area called Market Heights. My father was working at the massive Caterpillar plant. Mom had her hands full, with two other children, ages four and a half and 22 months.

One minute I was in the yard playing; the next minute I was gone. Mom frantically searched for me, and she finally found me a couple blocks away, sitting on a large rock in the middle of a small creek. She said I was just sitting there, watching the water. In retrospect, it seems maybe that little adventure was a foretaste of the rest of my life.

As a child I thought I would never grow old. Now that I am older, I am reminded of something once said by George Bernard Shaw: "Youth is wasted on the young." It does ring true, though tongue in cheek, but I really think God made it right. We *should* be tired and weary, when it comes our time to go home.

Broken Believer*

There was a man who reached out his hand
To make Jesus his Master and Lord
Soon he learned with life's every turn
God loved him more and more
  But he stumbled one day and wandered astray
  Far from God's shining truth
  He abandoned every prayer
  God was still holding on to

        So try to be strong, Broken Believer
        Please hang on, Broken Believer
Chorus: Let's get down on our knees; gather up every piece
        of your shattered faith
        Let God mend you today, Broken Believer

Now do you have a friend who's come to the end
of life's proverbial rope
Are you seeing signs they're leaving behind
Every sign of hope
  There is so little time
  You must let them know
  You can be a lifeline
  Should they let go

Repeat Chorus

"Broken Believer"
Words & Music written by Gary Owens ASCAP
Siler Creek Music ASCAP

*Dedicated to all broken believers.

251

Acknowledgments

This book is dedicated to my darling wife Dorothy and our two precious children, Christen Alexandrea and Justin Logan. Only God could have arranged for me to have such a precious family.

Thanks to our friend, Kayla Wood, for doing a lot of dedicated proof reading and editing.

Thanks to our wonderful friends, Ken and Teresa Glaskox, for urging me, many times over the years, to write down some of my life experiences. They are two of God's best encouragers.

Thanks to our dear friends, Buzz and Ouida Arledge. In the thirty plus years I have known them, they have been ever present as mentors, model Christians, and in many a storm ~ a lighthouse.